Henry T. Williams, Sophia Orne Johnson

Household Hints and Recipes

Henry T. Williams, Sophia Orne Johnson

Household Hints and Recipes

ISBN/EAN: 9783337403034

Printed in Europe, USA, Canada, Australia, Japan

Cover: Foto ©Lupo / pixelio.de

More available books at **www.hansebooks.com**

HOUSEHOLD

Hints and Recipes,

BY

HENRY T. WILLIAMS,
AND
"DAISY EYEBRIGHT."

PART I.

Williams' Household Series.
VOL. V.

NEW YORK:
HENRY T. WILLIAMS, Publisher.
1877.

Entered according to Act of Congress, in the year 1877, by
HENRY T. WILLIAMS,
In the office of the Librarian of Congress, at Washington.

CLARK W. BRYAN AND COMPANY,
ELECTROTYPERS, PRINTERS AND BINDERS,
SPRINGFIELD, MASS.

EDITORS' PREFACE.

COMMON SENSE is the richest endowment for every good housekeeper. In these pages are found some uncommonly good hints, which if observed will make *good housekeeping* a thing of pleasure, and sense and sentiment will more easily combine to make every home more delightful. In this volume there has been special effort to avoid the usual stereotyped "*Cook Book Recipes*" which have been repeated over and over again till all are familiar with them. Instead, something new, fresh, practical, sensible, has been furnished, which make a Ladies' Book of rare interest, and inestimable worth in every home. Every department of the house except the kitchen, will find here rare receipts and hints which will lead you to avoid a multitude of cares and annoyances, prevent many a serious accident, remedy many troubles, and save a waste of means. They are the result of personal experience of the Editors, and as such are intended to be strictly reliable and trustworthy.

Household Hints & Recipes

How to Keep Meat in Summer.

If you cover some putrid flesh with animal charcoal, such as is obtained by burning bones, you will utterly destroy all the bad odor, for it oxidizes the bad gases.

Now to what use can this be applied? You know how often it happens, particularly in the Summer, that the meat sent home on Saturday night for Sunday's dinner will become tainted, if the weather is hot and damp; sometimes it is so spoiled you cannot eat it. Yet it is quite sure that the process of decomposition that has gone on during the night has not been sufficient to render the meat unhealthy. There has no great putrefaction taken place. If you cover the meat with animal charcoal, and leave it all night, there will be no odor from it. And if you do not like to blacken it, you can easily have a small box made, and line it with the charcoal, powdered. Or, you can wrap the meat while it is sweet in a towel and put it in a box and fill the spaces up with animal charcoal, covering it also over the top with it; and place it in the ice-house or refrigerator. All musty smells can also be removed by its use.

A Cheap Filter for Water.

Take a large flower-pot, of porous substance, and place a piece of sponge in it, large enough to cover the bottom. Upon this put a few smooth white pebbles to keep the sponge in place, and fill up the pot, to within two or three inches of the brim, with a mixture of one part powdered charcoal, to two parts fine sharp sand. Cover the top of the pot with a piece of clean white flannel, tied tightly round the rim with a bit of twine, but not so closely that it will not sink down under pressure, in the center. Set the flower-pot over a pail, and pour the water into the flannel, letting it filter through the mixture, and by the time it has passed through the hole in the bottom of the flower-pot, it will be perfectly clear, and freed from all impurities.

To Render Cloth Fire-proof.

All cloth, even that for ladies' dresses of the most inflammable and lightest textures, can be made almost if not wholly incombustible, by being dipped into a weak solution of the chloride of zinc. Buy ten cents' worth of it, and put it into a quart or three pints of water, and dip in some pieces of muslin and woolen; when thoroughly dried, hold them over the fire, and see how slowly they burn, if at all.

To Prepare Fumigating Powder.

Take equal parts of cascarilla bark, in coarse powder, camomile flowers, and anise-seed, powdered and well mixed together. Two ounces of each will be sufficient to use for several times. Take up some hot coals upon a shovel, and sprinkle the powder over them very slowly; and as the smoke arises, carry the shovel into all parts of the room, and fumigate the air thoroughly. It destroys all disagreeable odors, and is said to prevent contagion in infectious diseases, such as diphtheria, scarlet fever, and the like.

A Disinfecting Lamp.

The following simple apparatus is most excellent for purifying rooms where any unpleasant effluvia prevails. Any person can fit up the lamp, and it is an agreeable method of overcoming bad odors in a sick room. Take a small glass lamp, such as is used for burning camphene or spirits, put in a clean wick, and fill it up with chloric ether and light the wick. In a few minutes the object will be accomplished.

In damp, dark cellars where vegetables have decayed, or where drains allow the escape of mephitic gas, in dissecting rooms, and in any place where it is desirable to sweeten the atmosphere, one of these lamps will prove most efficacious. One tube filled with a wick is quite sufficient.

To Purify Foul Apartments.

To one table-spoonful of common salt placed in a tumbler, add a large pinch of manganese, powdered fine. Turn over it a quarter of a wine-glass of strong vitriolic acid. Do this at an interval of a few minutes, four or five times; then place the tumbler on the floor of the room that requires fumigating, and leave it for a day or more, closing all the doors and windows tightly. The vapors formed by it will destroy all the foul odors, and sweeten the most filthy air.

An Excellent Disinfectant.

Permanganate of potassa in solution is one of the most efficient disinfectants that can be used for removing all disagreeable odors, either in utensils, or in rooms.

Twenty-five grains can be dissolved in two quarts of water, and a tablespoonful of it, added to a saucer of water, will remove any filthy odor. As the water evaporates more can be added to it. For infectious diseases it is highly recommended, and should always be used in all cases of scarlet fever, diphtheria, or small-pox.

For disinfecting mouldy barrels it is unequaled. Two or three table-spoonfuls of the solution, added to a pint of water, will cleanse any cask, or barrel, if it is thoroughly washed in it and rinsed out well.

A Method of Sweetening Musty Barrels.

Make a strong ley of hard-wood ashes, and pour it, boiling hot, into the bung hole; then roll the cask about so that every portion of it shall be well washed. If the first application does not sweeten it thoroughly, repeat it, and then rinse it out well with clear, hot water. If wood ashes cannot be obtained, fill the cask with hot water, and throw in small pieces of unslacked lime—a quart at least of it—shake it about well, and when nearly cold turn it out, and rinse it with clear water.

Or, mix half a pint of sulphuric acid in a quart of warm water, turn it into the cask, and roll it about so that it is all wetted. Let it stand over night, and the next day add a pint of powdered chalk, and let it effervesce; then bung it up for two or three days, and when it is rinsed, wash it out with boiling water. The filthiest cask can be cleaned in this manner.

How to Ascertain the Presence of Carbonic Acid Gas in the Atmosphere.

If the air of a room is foul, it can be readily ascertained by filling a glass tumbler with lime-water, and placing it on a shelf in the room. The rapidity with which a pellicle forms on its surface, or the water becomes cloudy, corresponds to the amount of carbonic acid present in the atmosphere that surrounds it. Another method is to place a little moist carbonate of lead on a plate or saucer, on the mantle-piece or shelf, and it will turn black if there is any sulphurated hydrogen in the air. This is a very delicate test for the destructive gas.

To Destroy Cockroaches.

A very simple trap can be prepared for these disagreeable pests by cutting four or five strips of paste-board, an inch or more in width, and placing them in a slanting position against the sides of a quart bowl or a common nappy. Then pour into the basin (taking care not to touch its sides) some molasses and water, or stale beer and molasses, and as cockroaches are very fond of sweets, they will walk up the ladders of paste-board, and find a watery death. Pieces of wood will do as well. Several of these traps can be placed in the kitchen and pantry, night after night, and soon their number will be greatly lessened. Another way is to place pieces of unslacked lime where the cockroaches frequent, and they will be driven away. But care must be taken not to let water drip upon the quicklime, as it would produce combustion.

Still another way is to take quantities of powdered borax, and scatter it all about the shelves and the water pipes. The cockroaches do not like it and will not run over it. A solution of alum in boiling hot water will destroy them at once and also kill their *larvæ*.

These insects always follow the water pipes in houses, but any of these simple remedies will keep them from putting in an appearance.

To Revive Old Writing.

Boil a few gall nuts in white wine, or alcohol; then with a sponge dipped in the liquid, wipe the lines of the almost invisible writing, very gently, and all the letters will appear distinctly visible. This preparation, however, should not be used for documents, of which the originals are the most valuable, as it has a tendency to injure, and eventually destroy the paper; but it is very desirable for manuscripts that you only desire to copy.

How to Become Thin.

The dietary that Banting observed to reduce his weight from 202 pounds to 150 was this: For breakfast, four ounces of beef, mutton or any kind of cold or broiled meat and fish, excepting pork, salmon, herring and eels; a large cup of tea without milk or sugar; an ounce of dry toast or a little biscuit, but no butter. For dinner, five or six ounces of any kind of meat or fish—excepting those prohibited; any vegetable excepting potatoes, beets and parsnips, with one ounce of dry toast; any kind of poultry or game, and ripe or cooked fruits; but no pastries, puddings or sweets are allowed. For tea, dry toast, a cup of tea without milk or sugar, and two or three ounces of fruit. For supper, three or four ounces of meat or fish, with a glass or two of claret or madeira. Food that contains sugar and starch must be avoided, as it creates flesh too rapidly. Take two or three hours' exercise daily, and retire and rise in good season.

HOUSEHOLD HINTS AND RECIPES.

How to Prevent Explosions of Gas.

We hear occasionally of severe accidents from the leakage of gas pipes, when light is brought into collision with the gas, and every one should know what to do to prevent the possibility of the occurrence. The first thing, when an escape is observed, is to turn the gas off at the meter, without taking a light to do it. Then open the windows in the rooms, at the top as well as at the lower part, because gas is light and ascends to the ceiling. Meanwhile, a gas-fitter should be sent for at once.

With a little attention, however, explosions of gas are barely possible. So disagreeable is its odor that an escape is perceptible at once when there is only one-three thousandth part present in the atmosphere, and no explosion can take place unless there is one part in fifteen. Therefore, it is chiefly in small rooms and closets that there is much danger in cases of escape of gas. The stop-cock near the meter should be turned several times in a year to prevent its corroding and not turning easily, when you desire to shut off the supply.

How to Obtain Sleep.

Sleep is the great panacea of earthly ills, yet it is a coy guest, and often has to be wooed long before it is won. But we would on no account recommend to our readers the foolish practice of trying to obtain sleep by the use of narcotics, which should never be resorted to except by the advice of physicians. Many are the patent prescriptions for sleepless nights—and onions—raw onions, sliced thin, and eaten with a bit of bread, are said by many to be a sure specific for the trouble.

A famous divine tells us that he could always obtain sleep by repeating very slowly, with a long inspiration and expiration at each vowel, the letters, A, E, I, O. The fifth vowel was omitted because it demanded too great an exertion of the muscles of the lips. Sleep would soon follow the mechanical repetition of the vowels above named.

Others tell us they can woo sleep by chaining the imagination to one object, for instance the watching a field of corn waving in the breeze, and seeing the sunlight glance upon its lance-shaped leaves. While others more prosaic, would see a flock of sheep jumping one after another through a hedge.

A Sure Remedy for Nervous Sleeplessness.

Take one or two sugar-coated assafœtida pills before retiring.

To Make a Pot-Pourri, or Scent Jar--No 1.

Take one ounce of gum benjamin, sweet orris, storax, cloves and nutmeg, all bruised in a mortar; throw in at the bottom of the jar, a handful of salt and a little of the mixture of spices; then add layers of rose leaves and other kinds of odorous leaves, and upon every layer add a handful of salt and some spices, taking care to cover every leaf with the salt and spices. The best materials for a *pot-pourri* are rose leaves, sweet briar, violets, lavender, rosemary, clovepinks, and in fact every sweet-scented herb or flower that you can obtain. Sweet geranium leaves and flowers, and sweet verbena leaves should never be forgotten.

Collect the flowers and leaves when in their prime, and pick them clean from the stalks. Keep it closely covered for three months, then stir it up with a stick, and its fragrance is delicious.

Pot-Pourri, No. 2.

Take of orris root and flag root, bruised, each four ounces, yellow sandal wood, three ounces, sweet cedar wood one ounce, half an ounce of cloves, one ounce each of gum benzoin, styrax and nutmeg powdered, mix all the ingredients together, and add one pound of fine bag salt, three ounces of rose leaves, half a drachm of essence of lemon, one drachm of *millefleurs*, twenty drops oil of lavender, ten grains of musk.

This powder is also excellent for perfuming linen, furs and woolen goods, and makes nice *sachet* powder if the salt and rose leaves are left out, and ten drops of otto of rose substituted. It will retain its scent for years.

To Loosen the Stoppers of Smelling Bottles.

If the stopper is firmly fixed by means of the salts contained within the bottle, do not attempt to strike out the stopper, but add as much citric acid to water as it will take up, thus making what chemists term a saturated solution, and immerse the neck of the bottle in it. Or you can pour some vinegar into a tumbler, and put the neck and stopper into that. In the former case a citrate of ammonia will be formed, and in the latter an acetate of ammonia. After the bottle has remained in the tumbler for ten minutes or so, remove it to a tumbler of warm water, and in a few moments it will come out readily

To Remove the Stoppers of Glass Bottles.

Dip a piece of woolen cloth into boiling hot water, and wrap it tightly around the neck of the bottle. In a few minutes the stopper will probably be loosened, as we have never known this method to fail.

To Clean Brass Andirons and Fenders.

Wash the brass with a strong solution of oxalic acid, and when dry, rub it until it shines like gold with cloths moistened with Sapolio. Or, dampen a cloth with kerosene, dip it into Tripoli, and rub very thoroughly. Polish with dry newspapers.

HOUSEHOLD HINTS AND RECIPES.

To Preserve Iron and Steel from Rust.

The preservation of iron and steel from rust is quite an important item in domestic economy, and the following method will never fail to do it: Add half a pound of quicklime to a quart of cold water. Let it stand until perfectly clear, and then pour off the liquid, ceasing the moment it becomes turbid. Stir into it enough olive oil, until the mixture becomes like a thick cream. Put it into a jar and keep it for use. Rub the article to be put by with it and then wrap it up in paper. Knives and all steel articles will not acquire the slightest rust if treated in this way. If they cannot be wrapped up in paper, add another coating of the mixture. Iron pans and kettles covered with it will not rust; and it is also a sovereign remedy for burns or scalds. Rub it over the affected spot at once, and blisters cannot form.

To Clean Common Tins.

Throw some wood ashes into a wash kettle, pour on water till it is nearly full and let it boil. Then dip in the tins, and leave them to boil about ten minutes. Take them out, one at a time, and scour while hot, with fine sand and soap. After soap has been made in a big brass kettle, it is a good plan to fill it half full of water, and let it boil up well, and throw in all the tin utensils; then scour them with a strong piece of crash dipped in sand and soap, or pure powdered whitening, as it will give a better polish. Rinse them in a tub of cold water, and set in the sun to drain. When dried, rub off with a thick woolen cloth, and they will look bright and nice. Pewter platters and dishes can be cleaned in the same way.

When wood ashes are not obtainable, take a cake of *Sapolio*, dampen a piece of flannel, and rub on it until you have a good suds. Scrub the tins with it, and they will shine like a mirror.

To Take Care of Handles of Knives.

Ivory or bone handles should be washed with a soaped flannel and lukewarm water, and then wiped dry. To preserve or restore their whiteness, soak them in alum water that has been boiled, and then become cold. Let them lie in it for an hour; then take them out, and brush them well with a soft tooth-brush, and wrap a soft linen towel about them, wetting it in cold water, and leaving them to dry gradually. If dried too quickly, when taken out of the solution of alum, it will injure them; but if properly managed this process will make them very white. Handles of ebony should be cleaned with a soft cloth, dipped in a little sweet oil. Let them lie in the oil for an hour, and then wipe it all off with a soft bit of flannel.

HOUSEHOLD HINTS AND RECIPES.

To Clean Plate Much Tarnished.

Take of alum, common salt, and cream of tartar, each one ounce; pulverize the alum, and dissolve the whole in one gallon of water. Boil it well, then put in the pieces of plate, and boil them for ten minutes. Take out and rub dry with chamois leather, wiping them at first with soft linen. If plate is put aside it will generally tarnish, but if cleaned by this method, at stated periods, it will always look bright.

To Prepare Cloths for Polishing Silver.

Take two ounces of powdered hartshorn, and boil it in a pint of water; soak small squares of linen cloth (pieces of old table-cloths will do), in the liquid, and hang them up to dry, without wringing, and they will polish silver beautifully.

To Clean Candlesticks, Snuffers, etc.

Silver plated and japanned candlesticks, snuffers, and snuffer-stands should be cleaned by first removing the drops of wax or tallow that may have fallen on them by pouring boiling hot water over them, and then wiping them dry with a linen towel, and rubbing them with chamois leather. But on no account place them before the fire to melt off the grease, as too much heat will injure the face of the plate. In placing candles in the sockets, fit them in closely, either by means of a strip of paper tightly twisted about them, or by the ordinary candle-springs; they will thus be prevented from jostling, and spilling the melted portion of the wax or tallow upon the tables and floors.

To Restore Alabaster Ornaments.

Make a mixture in the proportion of two ounces of aquafortis, or nitric acid, to a pint of cold rain water, which should be filtered, as it is necessary that the water should be perfectly clear. Dip a small paint brush into the liquid, and wash the alabaster for ten minutes, putting the brush into all the crevices, which should have been thoroughly brushed and dusted before being wetted. Rinse thoroughly with cold water, and set in the sun for two or three hours to dry. Do not wipe it off. The aquafortis will make the alabaster very white, and being used so weak it cannot injure it. Soap should never be put on to alabaster, as it discolors it badly.

To Give Plaster Figures the Appearance of Marble.

Dissolve one ounce of pure soda soap, grated fine, in four ounces of hot water; add one ounce of white wax shaved very thin. Put the mixture into an earthen dish, and when it is all melted to a liquid, warm the figure before the fire and tie a string around it so you can dip the whole of it into the mixture at once.

When the varnish has become well dried in, dip it a second time into the liquid. This is usually sufficient. Set the figure carefully away on a closet shelf excluded from all dust for a week. Then rub it gently and carefully with some soft cotton wool, and you will produce a brilliant gloss exactly resembling polished marble.

To Varnish Old Straw Hats and Baskets, Black or Red.

Take either red or black sealing-wax; to every two ounces of the wax, pounded very fine, and sifted through sheer muslin, add one ounce of rectified spirits of wine. Put it into a large white glass phial, and shake it for ten minutes. Then let it stand in a warm place for forty-eight hours, shaking it occasionally until all of the wax is dissolved. Put it on to the hats or baskets with a small painter's brush. Let it dry, and repeat the application, and your sunburned hats, and soiled baskets will be as good as new.

To Restore Faded Harnesses.

The color of a harness that has become rusty or brown by wear, can be restored to a fine black, after the dirt has been sponged off, by using the following mixture: Boil half a pound of logwood chips in three quarts of water, to which add three ounces of finely powdered nutgalls, and one ounce of pulverized alum. Simmer the whole together for half an hour, bottle when a little cooled, and apply with a soft brush or cloth.

An excellent blacking for harnesses is made by melting two ounces of mutton suet with six ounces of beeswax; then add one ounce of powdered indigo, five heaping table-spoonfuls of fine sugar, dissolved in half a teacup of milk, and two heaping table-spoonfuls of soft soap. Stir all together thoroughly; simmer over the fire until well mixed, and add one gill of turpentine as you take it from the fire. Lay on with a sponge; polish with a cloth and brush.

To Make Economical White Paint.

Two quarts of sweet milk, eight ounces of fresh slaked lime, eight ounces of linseed oil, two ounces of Burgundy pitch, three pounds of Spanish white. Slake the lime in a little water and expose it to the air. Stir it to a stiff paste with one pint of milk. Dissolve the pitch in the linseed oil; and then mix it slowly drop by drop into the whitewash, stirring carefully as you do in mixing a salad. Then stir in the rest of the milk, a little at a time, not the whole at once, as it will not mix smoothly; stir in the Spanish white. This quantity will cover twenty-seven square yards of surface, and prove a most economical paint.

Cheap Paint Impervious to Weather.

Dissolve eight pounds of glue in boiling water, and with this slake one bushel of quicklime until it becomes of the usual consistency of paint. Lay on three coats of this mixture with a painter's brush, taking care that each coat is dry before it is succeeded by another. Over the third dust sand, or stone dust from a dredger. By mixing ochre or Spanish brown with the wash other colors can be obtained. Mix common blue and yellow ochre and a handsome green wash can be made. Apply it hot, and you will find it excellent for fences, palings and outhouses.

How to Manage Household Expenses.

Of course, different people pursue different plans in managing their household expenses, but every one should keep an account of daily expenditures, and carry them out every month, and know at the end of the year just how they stand. And it is very essential that every woman who keeps house, should have a stated sum for the purpose, weekly or monthly, and take into consideration the occasional expenses to which she is liable—such as medical attendance, rent, coals, gas bills, servants' wages, clothes, and the like, and reserve from each week's expenditures a sufficient proportion towards paying these bills. Such moneys can be kept on interest in a savings bank as they are not needed for monthly expenses, as they are saved by a little economy exerted here and there. Going without dessert every day, or without meat every day for breakfast will amount to quite a little sum in six months or a year; and in due time enough might be saved by these little sacrifices to the stomach to send a daughter to school, or even pay a son's expenses at college.

"*Many a little makes a mickle*," is an old Scotch proverb that is particularly to be remembered and applied in housekeeping. And for want of it plenty is often consumed in prodigality, and distress and destitution ensue.

Home Economy.

We should never feel ashamed of whatever economy it is right for us to practice, but take a pride in its exercise; and if at any time we find ourselves endeavoring to conceal our thrift, it is time to pause and examine our motives; for we either desire to appear richer than we are, or else the economy in question is needless, and hence arises the shame. It is very possible, however, to arrange our households so judiciously that we spread a charm over a plain and, perhaps, even a homely establishment.

The accomplished Lady Mary Wortley Montague, who figured in the fashionable as well as in the literary circles of her time, said: " The most minute details of household economy become elegant and refined, when they are enobled by sentiment. To furnish a room is not then a commonplace affair, to be shared with upholsterers and cabinet-makers, but it is decorating a place where I am to meet a friend or a lover. To order dinner is not merely arranging a meal with my cook, it is preparing refreshment for him whom I love. These necessary occupations, viewed in this light by a person capable of strong attachment, are so many pleasures, and will afford her far more delight than the games and show that constitute the amusements of the world.

Spring House-Cleaning, and the Best Way to Arrange It.

When the balmy southern breezes have driven away the cold easterly winds, and the sun has crossed the vernal line and its bright rays enliven our winter-decked rooms, they will also disclose the blackening dust which has settled upon the walls, ceilings, curtains, etc., in spite of all our efforts to expel it; and every careful housewife is aware that the season is close at hand, when she must re-adorn and arrange her house from the attic to the cellar, and rout out the foul fiend—dirt—which one of our latter-day philosophers has termed " *matter in the wrong place.*"

There are few houses in the United States which do not undergo, at least twice a year, a thorough cleaning, and although it is by no means an agreeable operation when in process, yet when the work is completed, the disagreeableness of it is wholly forgotten in the pleasure we take in knowing that the house *is clean, smells clean* and *feels clean*; and that there is no dark cellar, or hidden corner, that is not as sweet and fresh as are the parlor, dining-room and kitchen.

But the first aim in house-cleaning should be to perform it with as little discomfort as possible to those of the household, who do not actively participate in it; and to do this the housekeeper must manage matters, so that the whole house is not in confusion at once; and not endeavor to accomplish too much, *i. e.*, not attempt to clean one story at a given time, but take it easily and not let chaos reign *everywhere*. This can easily be done by commencing with the cellar first, and then the attics, and next the chambers and closets, etc.; and taking up only as many carpets as can be put down in the same day, and thus have each room put in order before night, instead of having several in confusion, and no comfortable place in the house for either bipeds or quadrupeds to rest themselves. In this way, also, the dirt will not be trodden backwards and forwards, nor swept into the carpets and staircases by the servants' dresses.

If the gentleman of the house can be persuaded that the cleansing process can be accomplished more readily in his absence, he could probably be induced to enjoy a change of scene; and then the labors can go on without the hindrance of much cookery, which always consumes so large a portion of time in every household.

Painting, papering and whitewashing are the order of the day in Spring house-cleaning, and wherever they have sway, their claims upon one's time are all absorbing. . Yet after the work is finished to one's satisfaction, the annoyances one has been subjected to are slight compared to the enjoyment one takes in the fruit of their labors.

The unoccupied chambers should be put in order the first, and those rooms that are used the most, should be left until after the mud and dirt of unsettled roads are of the past, and less soil will be brought into the house. We will give in detail the *modus operandi*.

How to Clean a Room Thoroughly.

All the articles of furniture should be taken from their places, and if possible out of the room. If the chairs and lounge are upholstered, they should be thoroughly beaten with a furniture whip, such as are sold at house-furnishing stores. It can be made by lightly braiding or twisting together two or three rattans, and uniting the ends in a handle, and are an excellent article with which to beat out the dust from all furniture, mattresses, and carpets. After beating the two first articles they should be brushed over with a feather duster, and wiped off with a soft cloth.

If the furniture cannot be removed from the rooms, cover it with pieces of cotton, such as old sheets or table cloths. But the better plan is to purchase twenty yards of cheap cotton at four or five cents a yard—the cheapest made—and sew it together in strips like sheets, and keep them especially for the purpose of covering beds and furniture, not only in seasons of semi-annual, but also in weekly cleanings, taking care, however, to wash them occasionally. The pictures, draperies and blinds must then be taken down, dusted and cleaned. If it has been decided that the paperers and painters are not needed, do not neglect the whitewasher, for his work is very essential to the freshness of chambers; besides, the lime and water will destroy all the eggs of spiders and the like. Then the paper must be brushed over by fastening a white cloth over the top of a broom, and sweeping it down the wall in regular strokes, so as not to give it a streaked appearance. If the room is used for a sleeping room, take the bed to pieces, if possible, and wash all the unvarnished parts in boiling hot alum and water. This is sure death to insects of all kinds.

The grate and fire-irons must be black-leaded and rubbed bright. The paint washed, including the window-sashes, the windows cleaned, the floor scrubbed, the carpet well beaten, and the furniture polished. Then when the sunshine has aired and dried the room thoroughly, put down the carpet, and replace the furniture, and hang up the curtains, and rejoice in the beauty of your surroundings.

How to Clean Carpets.

Carpets should always be beaten on the wrong side first, and then very gently on the right side; and care should be taken not to use pointed sticks, as they are apt to tear holes in thin carpeting. Ingrain and three-ply carpets should be lifted every Spring, and if the room is used constantly, it is well to have them shaken in the Autumn also, as the dust and grit penetrates them easily, and helps to wear them out. If such a carpet can be shaken upon the crust of snow that often forms hard enough to bear a man, in the early Spring, it will be well cleaned. Then after it is laid on the floor, scatter snow over it, a little at a time, and sweep it off, and it will revive the faded colors. Brussels and velvet carpets do not need to be taken up oftener than once in two or three years; and the heavy Wiltons, Moquettes and Axminsters, not oftener than once in three or four years. Their fabric is so firm, that dust cannot sift through it, and a thorough sweeping will cleanse the surface. Then take two ounces of carbonate of ammonia to one gallon of water, and wring out a cloth in it, and rub it, breadth by breadth, all over the carpet. Wring out the cloth in the water at every yard, and if it becomes much soiled, procure a clean supply. If after a carpet has been well beaten and cleaned in this way, it still looks soiled, take a pint of ox's gall, which you can procure of your butcher, and turn it into three quarts of cold water, and rub it all over the carpet with a soft scrubbing brush. Rinse the lather off with clear cold water, and rub the carpet dry with a soft cloth.

In this climate we cannot do without carpets, entirely, yet their use in bedrooms is not productive of cleanliness, as they are liable to harbor vermin, dust and dirt. Rugs are now taking the place of carpets to quite an extent, and as they can be taken up and shaken easily, they recommend themselves to the neat housewife. A square rug in the center of the floor with a small one at the bureau, door and washstand will answer all the purposes of a carpet. If the floor is not well laid, however, it is well to put down matting, and then use the rugs. Or, the floor can be painted in a light gray or ash color, and a Grecian pattern, in vermilion, green, bright blue or brown painted all around the edges of it. A center piece could also be painted in the middle, and then varnished or oiled, so that it would keep bright for years. Tiles and inlaid woods are, of course, much more elegant for floors, and when the first cost is not to be closely consulted, they are really the cheapest floors that can be laid. If the planks of the floor are of the same width, they can be painted longitudinally in dark brown, leaving the other half the natural color; and when thoroughly dried, can be oiled, and in this way an ugly floor will look almost as well as if it were made of small boards of hard wood of two colors.

A square rug can be made of breadths of Brussels or of common carpeting, sewed together, and bordered with a bright bordering, sewed all round it; or a fringe can be made for it of woolen cloth cut in strips, and raveled out, and tied in knots.

When cleaning rooms in which the carpets are not taken up, be careful to spread over them some pieces of old drugget, or sheets of newspaper to keep them from injury. A stiff round, or pointed brush will be needed to brush out the dust that has collected in the corners, and along the wainscots.

How to Clean Wall Paper, and Walls.

Brush wall paper carefully with a feather duster, and with a cloth tied over a broom as previously directed. But if after dusting thoroughly they still look much soiled and grimmy, take half a loaf of very stale bread, moisten it a little on the cut surface, but only enough to dampen, not to wet it, and rub the wall, in a straight line, from the ceiling to the mop-board, very gently, and in this way go all over the paper. Common papers cleaned in this way often look very nicely, but the more expensive ones, gilded, etc., will not cleanse as well. If stale bread cannot be had, mix up a lump of flour and water, very stiffly, and use it, rubbing the wall softly, and taking the length of the arm at each stroke. Cut off the soiled part and in commencing the stroke go a little above where the last one ended, but be careful not to cross the paper, or rub up and down. It is well to try the paper first, behind a wardrobe or bureau, and see if it will clean well.

If there are any places where the furniture has broken through the paper and plaster, make a mixture of equal parts of plaster of Paris and silver sand, into a paste with a little water, and fill them up with a knife, smoothing off the plaster carefully. Cut some pieces of paper to match in exactly, and the patch will not be visible. Always save some of the paper of each room in the house for repairs, and if any place becomes soiled or defaced wet it with a strong solution of saleratus and water, when it will peel off readily. Then put in a new piece with a paste of flour and water, boiled like starch. If there are any spots of grease on the walls, mix some fuller's earth with a little ox-gall and cold water to a stiff paste, spread it on the spot and cover it with a little blotting-paper, and let it stand for three or four hours; then brush it off, and if any grease remains, put on some more of the paste, and proceed as before.

To Black-lead and Polish Grates.

Grates and fenders should be polished in every part, and if they have become discolored, Brunswick varnish made from the following recipe will restore the color: Melt half a pound of asphaltum gum in one pint of oil of turpentine, and when it has become well dissolved, stir into it a quarter of a pint of linseed oil. If it is too thick to run easily from the brush, add a little more turpentine. These materials can all be cheaply obtained, and make an excellent blacking for ranges as well as grates. Polished grates and irons must be rubbed with a dry leather every two days or so, and oftener in damp weather. If they have become dulled or rusted, rub them with emery paper, or if you cannot obtain that, mix equal parts of turpentine with sweet oil, and stir in enough emery powder to make a thin paste. Rub this on the steel with a piece of old flannel, rub off with another piece, and brighten with old newspapers, which are also excellent to brighten brasses and tins after they have been well scoured.

To Clean White Paint.

Neither soap, nor soda, nor ashes should be often used in cleaning white paint. Take a handful of finely powdered whiting on a plate, and have a piece of soft flannel, and a pail of warm—not hot water. Wet the flannel, squeeze it dry, dip it into the powder, and rub the paint up and down until it is clean; wash off with clear water, and rub dry with a soft cotton or linen cloth. If the paint is much soiled with coal dust, cigar smoke, etc., add a little bullock's gall to the whiting and it will come off readily. In washing the wainscot take great care not to touch the edge of the paper with the wet cloth, as it would injure its appearance.

To Clean Wainscots and all Painted Woods Much Soiled.

Four ounces of potash and four ounces of powdered quicklime should be mixed together, and three quarts of boiling water poured over it. Let it boil in an iron kettle for half an hour. Let it stand until it is cold and well settled. Pour off the clear liquid and dip a painter's brush into it, and pass it over the surface of the wood in the same way as in painting. Wipe it off at once with a flannel wet in cold water. This mode of cleaning will frequently render a new coat of paint unnecessary; and it has the advantage of being destructive to the eggs of all kinds of insects, which may be deposited in the crevices of the wainscot. When you suspect that such *larvæ* are present, as an additional precaution, add two drachms of corrosive sublimate to the mixture, and not a cockroach or chintz bug will venture forth.

To Clean Colored and Varnished Paints.

Save the tea grounds for several days before house cleaning. Then boil them up in considerable water, for half an hour. Strain off the water, and add to it one table-spoonful of powdered borax. Take a soft flannel cloth and dip into it, squeeze it almost dry, and wash the paint with it, first letting it become nearly cool. This will take off all smoke, dust and fly-specks, and give to varnished paint a bright, new look, while it does not injure the paint at all. Do not wet a large surface at once, so that it becomes dry before it is rubbed dry, for if you do, you will be obliged to go over it again. Careless wiping of paint will give it a streaked look.

How to Clean the Cellar.

This part of house cleaning is often neglected, and yet it is of the greatest importance, for unless it is free from foul odors, no part of the house can be healthful. If coal is used, as is most generally the case, the first step is to remove all the ashes, after they have been well sifted; and as they make an excellent mulch for currants, raspberries, gooseberries, etc., they should all be put on the garden. But if you are not the fortunate possessor of one, and the ashes have accumulated, instead of being removed daily, they should be carted away, or spread upon the street.

Have all the empty barrels, boxes, and the like, chopped up into kindling wood, if they are not desirable for other uses. And now is the best time to replenish the coal bins before the Spring cleaning occurs, as it cannot be put into the cellar without leaving its traces in other parts of the house; and it is usually to be obtained at as low a price in the Spring as in the Autumn when the demand for it is much greater. Shut the registers in every room when putting in coal or removing ashes. The furnace should be thoroughly cleaned and the pipes brushed out and renewed if needed. Then sweep down all the dust and cobwebs from ceiling and walls. Carry out all the decaying vegetables; look into the pork and beef barrel, and see that their contents are in a proper condition.

Take half a bushel of quicklime, and ten pounds of copperas; dissolve the latter in five gallons of boiling water; when it has melted, stir it into the lime. A firkin is a good thing in which to mix it. Stir it up well; the copperas makes it a light yellow. With a whitewash brush wash over the ceiling and walls. Let one coat dry well, and then put on another. It will sweeten the foulest cellar, and will also drive out all kinds of vermin—even rats will flee before its cleansing influences.

Dissolve ten pounds of copperas in five or six gallons of water, and wash all the wood work with it, shelves, etc., and also the floor, and you will have the sweetest cellar you have ever seen.

It was tried in an old house whose walls were filled with rats, and a great stampede followed. Two cats could not devour all the rats that were running away; while the neighboring barns and outhouses were filled with them. Copperas turns lime of a yellow shade, but it does not look badly on the cellar walls.

To Clean Beds and Bedding.

Take off the bedding, and carefully examine the mattresses and bindings while you brush out all the dust from their corners and sides with a painter's brush. Then carry them out into the yard and lay them on the dry grass, or put them on the roofs of the piazza, and beat them very thoroughly, wiping off the dust with a soft cloth, and cleaning out the tufts that tack them together, with the little brush. If there are traces of the chintz bug, dissolve quarter of a pound of alum in enough boiling water to hold it in solution, perhaps half a pint will do it. Dip in your brush and rub it along the bindings and through the corners and into the tufts of the mattress, and no *larvæ* can hatch out. If, however, these pests are quite numerous take a little powdered Paris green in a dredging box, and shake it wherever one could hide in the mattress.

Wash the wood of the bedsteads with the boiling hot alum, and smear the joints with a mixture of soft soap and red pepper, and no bugs can harbor there. Use the Paris green with caution, as it is a poison; so do not inhale it, but hold the head away as you shake the dredger.

To Clean Windows and Mirrors.

Windows are difficult to keep clean at all seasons of the year, for the dust of the streets as well as of the house lodges upon them, and even while cleaning it is blown over them. But a soft paper dipped into a little alcohol will cleanse them quickly, and give a better polish to the glass than water, while soap-suds and a soft cloth can never clean glass so that it looks well, for there will be traces of lint, do the best you may, and the newspaper can all be rubbed off, easily, if not moistened too much. In the Winter and early Spring, alcohol and water will be the best thing to use. But cold tea, prepared as directed for cleaning varnished and colored paint, will also take off fly-specks and smoke as quickly and give almost as good a polish. Dip a handful of newspapers into it, and rub the glass carefully up and down, not zigzag, and across corners. Then wipe it dry with another piece of paper. Mirrors can be cleaned by the same process. After you have once tried it you will never allow any other method to be pursued. To clean the corners of the windows, use the painter's brush, or tie a bit of flannel around a stick.

To Wash Floors.

When painted floors are washed often, it is best to mop them up with weak soap-suds, but if they are unpainted, sand and warmish water alone are better, as soap and soda blacken rather than whiten plain wood. Fuller's earth and silver scouring sand made into a paste and rubbed over boards will also whiten them. It should be sprinkled over the floor, and be well scrubbed in the direction of the grain of the wood, then washed off with lukewarm water. If the floor be spotted with grease, mix a quarter of a pound of pearlash with one pint of hot water, and scrub the floor with it, and a little sand. Some white wood ashes from the fire-place will answer the same purpose.

To Clean Door-Knobs, Bell-Pulls, and Speaking-Trumpets.

Cut a hole in a piece of soft oil-cloth, and put it around the knob or bell-pull, and it will protect the paper or paint from being soiled with the Sapolio, or whiting. Wet a flannel, rub on the Sapolio, and polish the knob. Rub dry with chamois leather.

To Clean Pictures and Chromos.

Brush the frames with a soft brush, and blow the dust out of any crevices which cannot be touched in any other way. Clean the glass with pieces of newspaper wetted in alcohol, or in cold tea, and be careful to wash them straight, beginning always at the top and going down to the bottom, and taking heed not to touch the gilt moulding or frames. If the frames require restoration, dissolve as much flour of sulphur as will give the required yellow tinge, in about a quart of water, and boil half a dozen small onions, cut in slices, in the liquid until they are tender. Strain the liquid, and when it is quite cold, wash the frames with it, and let them dry without wiping off.

To clean colored chromos, wet a cloth in a little cold tea, do not have it too wet, only dampened, and rub up and down until every fly-speck has disappeared; then wipe it off with a piece of chamois. If they are very much discolored, after washing as directed above, take a little bit of olive oil on a soft leather, and polish the surface.

To Clean Venetian Blinds.

Unfasten the tape at the bottom of the blind, and draw out all the laths. Wash them with lukewarm water and a very little soap, or with cold tea, and dry them thoroughly. When put up again take care that the cords which come down in the middle of the tapes are put in properly, as, if it is not attended to, the narrow tapes will fray.

To Clean Oil-Cloths.

Oil-cloth should not be washed in soap-suds or scoured with a brush, because it rubs off the paint, and fades the colors. Wash them with lukewarm water and a soft flannel, wipe perfectly dry. Then take sweet skimmed milk, and wipe the oil-cloth with it. By this way it can be kept clean and bright and will also last much longer. When oil-cloths have become dulled with soap-suds, take a little common varnish and a small brush, and varnish them all over. Of course they must not be trodden upon until the varnish has hardened well. Linseed oil will do as well as varnish.

To Make a Kitchen Oil-Cloth.

If you have a worn-out tapestry or Brussels carpet, you can make an excellent oil-cloth for the kitchen. Spread it wrong side outwards in the barn or on the grass, and paint it all over with any color you may fancy—light gray, Spanish brown, blue, green, or the like. Let it dry hard, then add a second coat; let it harden, and varnish with common varnish. This will make a far better oil-cloth than you can buy. Any painter will furnish the paints, and prepare them with reference to the work.

To Protect the Edges of Oil-Cloths.

All housekeepers who use pieces of oil-cloth to spread under stoves and in front of fire-places, know how liable the edges are to fringe or ravel out, and tear up. It matters not how strongly they may be nailed, they will become an eye-sore; and even when braid is used it soon wears out, and the resources of the house fail to furnish something durable and strong. This can be found, however, in strips of zinc, cut one and a half inches in width, and in lengths to correspond with the sides of the oil-cloth. Fold the parallel edges of the strips neatly together, insert the edges of the oil-cloth, and secure it by copper rivets. When well done the contrast between the bits of bright copper and the zinc is pleasing to the eye, while it will make one piece of oil-cloth outlast two put down in the common way.

To Make a Cheap Carpet.

Sew together strips of cheap cotton cloth, to match the floor you desire to cover; make a stiff rye flour paste with a little powdered borax or alum in it. And paste upon it sheets of wall-paper of some bright small pattern. Paste one strip at a time, smoothing it down carefully with pieces of old cotton. When it has dried perfectly, and presents an even surface, take some common varnish, and with a large brush, varnish the whole surface. Let it dry hard, then varnish again. Thus prepared it can be washed like oil-cloth, and wiped over with skimmed milk; and it will keep a good gloss, and if not hardly used, make a serviceable carpet for years.

How to Use Old Carpets.

Many a good rug can be made out of the unworn portions of the breadths of an old carpet. For greater durability they can be lined with old drilling, tow-cloth, parts of old sheets, or pieces of the same carpet that are more worn out. Sew the edges together and bind with a piece of carpet binding. Points of bright colored cloth two inches deep also make a pretty border; two rows in different colors can be sewed on to lap over the other. A good strong edge can be made of rows of braided woolen stuffs. If the center of a braided mat is made of a pretty piece of carpet it is a great improvement to it, and does not take nearly as many yards of braid to make a rug.

Pieces of carpet that are not large enough to cover rugs will make nice little crickets or stools, or boxes for holding slippers, rubbers, etc., or old newspapers for kindling fires. A large box to hold wood or coal can be covered with carpeting, and also make a good seat by placing hay or straw on the top of it, and covering it with batting, then tacking over it some strong cotton cloth, and again covering with the carpet. If neatly covered and cushioned, the box is not out of place in a dining-room, and is an excellent receptacle for the table linen of all kinds. Another can be made to hold the sheets and pillow-cases in a sleeping room. Shoe, soap, starch and salt boxes can all be made available in this way. Strong iron hinges can be placed upon the backs and lids, or straps of leather, nailed longitudinally to each, can do duty for them. If there is not enough old carpeting on hand, chintz or *cretonne* will answer your purpose, and add decidedly to the comfort of your surroundings.

How to Air Beds.

The most effectual way to air beds and bed clothing is to throw the clothes over a chair, and lift the mattress partly over the foot board in a round hoop like fashion, and if a feather bed is used pull it off upon a chair. Then open the windows and door so that a current of air can pass through the room, and let it remain so for two or three hours, or even longer. Beds thus aired are always healthful, and will induce sound sleep in their occupants. Each member of the family should be trained to do this daily, and never allowed to leave the room until it is so arranged. Boys as well as girls can be taught to do this, and they will reap the benefit of it through their lives, and be sure to have their children trained in the same way.

A bed that is only aired occasionally must contract impurities from the body and cannot be fresh and sweet. Some persons hang the pillows out of the windows, and it is an excellent plan, if you will first brush off the dust on the sill.

Mosquito and Fly Nets.

Those of our readers who can purchase fine woven wire in good hard wood frames need no directions for securing their windows and doors against the entrance of these annoyances. But for the million we would recommend mosquito-netting that can be bought in white, pink or blue, and any man or boy who can use a jack-knife and a hammer and nails, can make a suitable frame to fit any window. With the aid of a plane, nice strips of wood can be made, and if they are dove-tailed together at the corners, and then nicely painted a dark red, they will last many years. Lacking these appliances, however, common lath can be made to answer your purpose. Cut two strips to fit the width of the window, a little short to give room for the netting, and two more the length of the open window for the uprights. Nail these firmly together at the corners, and cover the frame with netting, either pasting it on, or nailing tightly. Mosquito netting can also be nailed over the window sashes on the outside of the frame. Frames for doors, with a support through the middle and hung upon the inside of the house with strong hinges, or simple straps of leather, and covered with the netting, are of great comfort to the housewife during the heated term.

How to Repel Moths.

Moths seldom touch cotton fabrics, but they delight to cut their way through woolen articles, and even a casing of leather is of little avail as a protection. But if the moth miller cannot find entrance to deposit her eggs, there is no danger from their ravages. If the crevices of a floor have become filled with them, dissolve half a pound of alum in boiling water, and wash every part of the mop boards, and fill up the seams between the boards with powdered borax, and few, if any of the eggs will hatch out. Wrap a cloth around a pointed stick and wet it in the hot alum water and wash out the corners of the floor, for it is there that the millers often deposit their eggs.

If moths are in the carpet, and you do not like to take it up, wet towels of common brown crash, in the hot alum water, and lay it wherever their ravages appear, and place a moderately hot flat-iron over it, letting it steam into the fibre of the carpet. It will not injure the wool, or the colors, but the heat and the alum will surely destroy all the *larvæ*.

In furnace-heated houses moths are constant in their depredations, and whenever you see a miller flying about, you must strive to kill it; but the gas-light or a candle will lure many to destruction. As early as possible in the Spring, powdered borax should be scattered wherever the moths are at work. To be sure nearly every housekeeper has her pet remedy for these pests, and some use red or black pepper, or sandal-wood, or camphor, or Persian powder. A strong odor is not liked by the millers, and therefore they do not select their nests in such places. Kerosene is particularly disagreeable to them, but as it is also to nearly every biped, we could not recommend its use.

If all woolen garments, etc., are done up in tight newspaper packages, and packed away in drawers, on top of which camphor gum and borax are sprinkled, one need have little occasion to trouble about them, unless the eggs were in the garments when thus packed away. Therefore, it is well to hang woolen garments upon the clothes line some bright windy day, and whip them with a riding whip or a rattan. Then fold them up, and put them away at once.

How to Take Care of Furs.

Some ladies think that when Spring comes, if they put away their furs, with care, in a camphor trunk, or wrapped tightly in old newspapers, and then in pillow-cases, with plenty of powdered camphor, black pepper or moth powder mixed in, they have done all that is requisite. But furs should first be carefully brushed the right way of the fur with a soft brush, and then an old linen or silk handkerchief should be folded smoothly over them, instead of the stiff paper that mats the fur; gum camphor, or any of the moth repellers can then be scattered over them, and the boxes can be hung up in pillow-cases or bolster covers, tied around with a string. More harm, however, is often done to furs by wearing them when the sun shines warm in the early Spring, than during the whole of the Winter, for it soon makes them shabby.

Prevention Against Moths in Clothing and Furs.

A very pleasant perfume for woolen clothes and furs, and a preventive against moths, can be made by the following recipe: Take one ounce each of cloves, cinnamon, mace, nutmeg, caraway seeds, and Tonquin-beans, add their whole weight in orris root; grind the whole to the finest powder, and put it in little bags among your bureau drawers and boxes of clothing. This will expel all moth millers. The best protection to furs is to beat them lightly with a rattan, then scatter this powder over them slightly, and do them up in newspapers, pasting their corners securely together. Put in a box or bag, scatter the powder in the top of it, and not a moth will ever enter there.

The Plague of Ants.

As the warm days come on in Summer, the plague of ants commences, and the housewife finds her closet and pantry shelves covered with tiny red and black ants, and larger black ones will also soon appear and infest every drawer and shelf. Chalk is an antidote against them. Take a large piece and draw a thick, broad mark all around the cupboard shelves, going over it again and again to deepen it. Draw the same half inch line on the edges of the sugar barrels or buckets, indeed, everywhere that they incline to congregate. If they are very thick upon the shelves, wet a large sponge, and sprinkle powdered sugar over it, and dip it every morning into boiling water, squeezing it nearly dry, and setting the trap again. In this way every ant will be expelled. Red pepper scattered plentifully over the shelves will also drive them away; and it is said that leaves of wintergreen, or young ivy, or of walnut trees, if laid upon the shelves and on the floors of pantries will rid them of the plague. Powdered alum or borax will drive away all the large black species.

An Home-made Refrigerator.

Nearly all housekeepers who are not able to obtain a refrigerator, keep their ice wrapped up in bits of old carpeting or some non-conducting material, which wastes the ice, and affords no help in preserving food. To them these directions may offer attractions: Take two large wooden boxes — dry goods boxes for instance—select the second one about a couple of inches smaller on all sides, and bore a one-inch hole in both, correspondingly, to give drainage and ventilation. Perhaps a couple of holes would do better. Fill up the space under the boxes with powdered charcoal or coal ashes. Put the inner box in place, and fill up all the spaces with the same. Saw-dust might do if nothing better is procurable, yet it is apt to become musty. Fix on the lids to both boxes to fit tightly, with iron hinges, (leather ones can be substituted,) and fasten with straps of leather, or a lock and key. Put shelves on each side of the inner box by means of cleats. Leave a place in the center for the ice. This is a rough refrigerator, to be sure, but far better than none. A zinc lining, or one of felting, would improve the inner box. A rack made of lathing can be laid at the bottom for the ice to rest upon. Legs can be added to the outer box by putting pieces of wood at each corner, and the drainage and ventilation will be improved; and an ingenious man can make an excellent ice box in this way.

Hints on Dress-making.

Thanks to various fashion books and pattern dealers, the housewife need not always await the leisure of the village dress-maker, but can select a suitable pattern, and do the cutting, fitting and making at home, which in these days of high priced dress-making, is a great saving in the household expenses. Yet to the inexperienced a few rules may not come amiss.

It is often well to lay your cloth out upon the floor or table, after the skirt has been duly cut, and plan the cutting of it, seeing where the sleeves can come out, and how the various pieces will fit one into the other. But to do this it is sometimes needful to smooth out the patterns with an iron.

Then look to see if the fabric has an up and down figure, and a right and wrong side, and arrange the patterns accordingly. If it possesses neither, it can be cut out of less cloth, because the gores can be matched in better, and it can be turned either way. Have a small saucer to hold the pins, sharp scissors, and a tape measure. Be careful to see that opposite sides of figures, stripes or plaids match alike, in backs and fronts of the body. Have both side forms of the same size, and let the strain at the bottom of the waist come exactly on the straight cross-ways of the cloth.

The outside seam of a sleeve at the top should always be the straight way of the goods. The inside seam should come exactly in the center of the arm-size, and the upper part of the front of the sleeve should curve sharply, and be at least three inches above the under side at the top, and it should be held a little full in seaming in, and sewed on the inside of the sleeve.

Puffs and ruffles, with few exceptions, should be cut on the perfect bias; bands, folds and pipings always on the bias, or cross-ways of the cloths.

In seaming a skirt begin at the top when possible and sew down, and hold the bias side of the gores towards you. If not possible, commence by pinning the gores together at the top, and sew from the bottom. In sewing up a shoulder seam hold the front very tight, pulling it firmly, from half way up the neck, then hold the back tightly the rest of the way. It is well to commence to baste it in the center. This way will prevent many wrinkles.

If one is stout take up a pleat, in the lining, at the button-holes, parallel with the front bias, also one under the arm on the front part of the basque, taking it in a slanting direction. Silk makes the best linings, and parts of old skirts can be used; the next best is tailor's drilling or jean. Black linen makes a good lining for black dresses that pull on the seams. Boil the linen in spent suds after the washing is over, rinse thoroughly in strong bluing water, and iron while quite damp. It is a very durable lining, and will last longer than two silk linings.

Whalebones should always be split in two, for if stiff they do not curve into the figure. Woolen braids should be shrunken in boiling water, before putting on to the dress. Shoulder and arm seams should be turned to the front to avoid drawing. For scant ruffles allow one-quarter or one-third of the fullness. For knife plaits allow three times the length of the skirt or polonaise.

From the middle of the front the skirt should slope gradually to the first seam, which should be a short inch longer than the skirt in front. For a stout figure make a little seam at each side of the front gore, or breadth. Waterproof cloaks should always be cut on the bias in the center of the back, as it prevents the ungraceful drooping at the sides after the cloth has been wetted.

If you use stiff linings for waist bodies, pull it out as much as possible, and iron smoothly before cutting out the pattern.

Plain Needlework.

Every girl should learn how to cut out, and make her own underclothing, and although it takes some little ability to become a skilled workwoman, yet if one perseveres, in the end, the trade will be obtainable by all. A seamstress has often not been taught to cut out, and you are forced to handle the scissors, if not to do the sewing. But in these days of paper patterns, every one can be taught to cut, although the gift of good fitting is not always obtainable, as forms differ so essentially; and a good cut for underclothing is only second in importance to a good cut for dresses and outside garments.

In teaching young girls to cut and sew, buy the soft undressed cottons, and let them see you cut out one garment; and then try to pin the pattern and cut it themselves. A little study into the matter will often enable you to save cloth, and therefore, it is well to lay it out upon a large table, or on the floor, and see how it can be cut to the best advantage. Let the beginner try to cut evenly, with long strokes of the scissors; and then try to sew evenly, also. Perfection in cutting and sewing will not come at once, but it can be attained; and, however wealthy you may be, you will never find that a knowledge of plain needlework is to be despised, for if it serves no other purpose, it will teach you how hard it is to become an adept in the art.

Flannels.

It is a good plan to shrink all flannels before they are cut out, by dipping them into quite warm water, and rinsing in lukewarm water. Wring them through the wringer, and dry quickly, in the sun, or by the range. All flannel clothing should be gathered, if any fullness is desired, rather than plaited, because in the latter case, they become thick and matted in washing and wearing; and in the event of their being turned, from top to bottom, in order to alter the wear, the part that had been plaited will be found so much injured, that it cannot be used. Under-flannel garments should be changed very often, as they imbibe perspiration, and become injurious to the health rather than a preservative.

Hints for the Laundry.

Machinery holds the same relation to washing that it does to sewing, *i. e.*, it does the work expeditiously, and with a great saving of labor, but it does require knowledge and experience to make it available, so that in the hands of the ignorant it will not always give satisfaction.

In selecting a washing-machine, the simplest are the most desirable, because they subject the clothes to less friction. But a wringer is a necessity for every one, as it saves so much manual labor. Soft water is also essential, and an abundant supply of hot and cold water, with two or more tubs, according to the size of your family.

Articles for the laundry should be sorted over, and dirty towels and greasy cloths kept apart from fine clothing; while colored things and flannels should always be washed separately. It saves the clothes and also labor to put them in lukewarm water over night, rubbing the most soiled portions, such as bindings to shirts and wristbands. The soiled articles should always be laid at the bottom of the tub. All white clothing should be washed in two waters; then boiled, and rinsed twice, once from the soap-suds, and then in bluing water.

Washing fluids, which are composed of lye, or sal-soda and lime, are injurious to white cotton fabrics, and should never be used for colored clothes. In the hands of experienced washerwomen they are, however, often of service, but if used by the ignorant washerwoman, too large a quantity is often taken to save labor, and of course the clothing must suffer. The practice of using lye to whiten clothes, while boiling, is particularly injurious, as it always decays the fabric.

The Use of Borax.

Borax is of the greatest use in the laundry, and as it does not affect the fabric of the cotton, or injure the hands of the washerwoman, we would recommend it highly. When it is mixed with sal-soda it renders it deleterious, and the following is an excellent washing fluid for all white articles.

Washing Fluid.

One pound of sal-soda and one pound of borax, dissolved in six gallons of warm water. When cold add five ounces of salts of tartar. Put the fluid into jugs or bottles. When used add one table-spoonful of it to every two gallons of water in which the clothes are soaked over night. Next morning wring them out, and turn the water into the boiler, and when hot enough, pour it over the clothes, and wash them with soap, adding more water as required. It takes much less soap when this fluid is used. When putting the clothes on to boil, add two table-spoonfuls of it to the suds. Once used the washerwoman will always desire it, as it finishes the work more satisfactorily.

Recipe for Bluing.

One ounce of Prussian blue; half an ounce of oxalic acid. Put in a bottle and add one quart of rain-water. Be sure the water is very soft, or the ingredients will not dissolve entirely. This is the cheapest and best bluing in use. It can be filtered through blotting-paper if it leaves any sediment.

To Wash Laces and Muslins.

Laces and muslins must never be rubbed in washing. Take a bar of white soap and shave off a little of it into enough hot water to dissolve it, and when cold it will be like a jelly. Mix a little of it with tepid water, and let the lace, etc., lie in it over night, then add a little boiling water and squeeze them repeatedly through the hands, so as to wash them, but do not rub them, as that will wear out the fabric. Lay them in a deep nappy, or small tub, and rinse them again and again in clear water, then set them in the sun, still in water, to whiten the laces. If the laces or muslins are small put them in a glass preserve jar, with a little soap in the water, and set it outside the window in the sun, until it has become sufficiently bleached.

To give lace and muslins that light, transparent look which new articles possess, mix the starch with a little cold water, mashing it with a spoon till quite smooth, then add more water until it looks like milk and water. Boil it in a yellow nappy until it is clear. Let it cool, and when comfortably warm to the hands, put in the laces and muslins, and squeeze out gently; then put them in a soft cloth, and squeeze as dry as possible. Take out each article by itself, and beat it between the palms of the hands to clear the starch from it. Fold up in a damp towel, as soon as the beating is over.

In doing up laces and muslins to look well, a great deal depends upon the ironing. First, the table should be covered with several thicknesses of soft blanket, because if it is hard the embroidery will be flattened too much, and a thin soft linen cloth should be laid on the blanket. In spreading out the article to iron, see that it lies perfectly even, so it will not look wispy when finished. The iron must be rubbed over dry salt, or with a bar of soap, and then polished on a cloth, so that it will not stick to the starch; or be too hot to scorch the lace. Scorching is a common fault with the inexperienced ironer, and it is a very bad one, for it leaves a stain that is ruinous to clear starching, and sometimes it is too deep to be removed without rotting the fabric. A little practice, however, in handling irons, will soon teach you the proper degree of heat, and until you have learned it, it is well to have an old napkin or bit of cloth with which to try the iron, before it is put over nice laces, etc.

If the starch sticks to the iron, fold up several thicknesses of newspaper, and rub a little beeswax over the flat-iron, and then rub it upon the paper until all grease is removed. This is an excellent precaution in ironing shirts.

How to Iron Shirts, Skirts, Vests, etc.

A bosom board is a needful adjunct to the iron table, and it can be made of well-seasoned pine, one inch thick, or a little more will do, eighteen inches in length, and twelve in width. Cover it with several thicknesses of an old blanket, stretching it over on one side, and tacking it firmly. Cover this with two thicknesses of Canton flannel, fleecy side up, nailing it with upholsterer's tacks, so as to hold it firmly. On the nailed side, spread a layer of thick paste made with wheat or rye flour, and stretch over it a piece of Canton flannel, and when it dries, paste on another and another until you have five thicknesses of the cotton—letting each one dry thoroughly before another one is added. The last one can be made to cover the edges of the others, and be nailed on to the side of the board with brads. The hard side will give a good polish to cuffs, collars and shirt bosoms, while the soft side will iron Marseilles vests and embroideries beautifully. Over the whole board put a thin cotton or linen cloth, an old pillow case will do, and baste it on so that it can be removed when soiled.

A skirt board is indispensable for ironing dresses and under skirts, and it should be about five feet and a half in length; eighteen inches in width, at the bottom, and ten inches at the top, where it can be rounded to three inches. Cover as directed for soft side of bosom board, and on the under side nail coarse cotton, so as to make it smooth to draw the skirts over it. Make a cover out of fine old cotton, and change as frequently as it becomes soiled.

In ironing a shirt, commence at the neck, and iron the binding, then fold the back in the middle, and press it smoothly, and iron the sleeves and wristbands; then iron the flaps, leaving the bosom and collar to the last. Slip in the board, rub the bosom over lightly with a damp cloth, and iron quickly and hard. A polishing iron with round edges is the best for this purpose, and also for vests, caps, etc., because it leaves no marks of the iron, and gives a better gloss. To iron a shirt collar, pass the iron rapidly over the wrong side, then iron the band, lastly the right side, which should be ironed and polished until perfectly dry and stiff.

Gentlemen's summer pantaloons should have a board made to fit them, loosely, and covered like a skirt board, and then they can be made to look well. Iron the pockets by turning them on the outside, before putting the board into the pantaloons.

To iron a skirt slip the small end through by the gathers, and iron breadth by breadth. A large piece of mosquito netting is very useful to keep the ironed clothes free from dust and flies, while being aired.

To Clean Colored Fabrics.

Nearly all colored fabrics stain the water used to cleanse them, and that without always losing their own brightness. No article of a different hue must be put into a wash or rinse so stained, but must have fresh water; and no colored fabric but black or blue must be rinsed in blued water. Different colors are improved by different substances being used in the wash or rinsing water. Sugar of lead will fasten all colors, and can be used, whenever they are likely to run. A ten cents' worth of it is enough for four or five gallons of water. Ox-gall will brighten all colors, no matter what is the fabric. For buff and cream-colored cashmeres, etc., mix in both waters a little of friar's-balsam. For black materials use *aqua ammonia* in suds and rinsing water; for violet and purple, the same. For green, put two table-spoonfuls of vinegar to every quart of rinsing water. For blue, a good handful of salt in the rinsing. For brown and gray, ox-gall. For white, blue the water.

To Wash Muslin Dresses.

Muslin dresses of the most delicate hues can be cleaned in quarter of an hour or less, without losing their color. Melt half a pound of bar soap in a gallon of water, by shaving it up thin, and empty it into the wash-tub. Have two other tubs of clean water at hand, and into one of them stir a quart of bran. Put the muslin into the soap-suds, when the water is comfortably warm to the hand, turn it about and squeeze it a little—letting every part become well wetted, and knead it in the water for a few minutes. Do not wring it at all, that injures its fabric, but squeeze it out of the suds, and put it into the bran water, and rinse it up and down quickly for a couple of minutes. Rinse it in the same way in the clear water. Squeeze it out, and hang between two lines, the neck of the waist or the binding of the skirt, if made separately, on one line, and the hem of one-half of the skirt on the other.

A clear, dry day should be chosen to wash muslin dresses, and several can be done at once. While the dress dries make the starch; if the muslin is colored, use cold starch; if white, make it as for shirt bosoms, stirring it about with a wax candle. Dip the dress into it; hang it again, to dry. When dry, rinse it quickly, but thoroughly, in clear water. Hang it out to dry again. Sprinkle, and roll it tightly in a towel. Iron with very hot irons, but not so hot as to scorch. Hot irons keep the stiffness in the muslin. Percales, cambrics and madras suitings, can be washed in the same way, but they will need to be rubbed more than muslins. The advantages of thus cleaning colored dresses are, that it is so quickly done that there is no time for the colors to run; and the fabrics are not strained and worn out. When sugar of lead is used, let the dress soak in the water for half an hour or more. Be careful not to use it, if there are scratches or abrasions on your hands.

A Convenient Soap Dish, Etc.

A great deal of soap is often wasted for want of a receptacle to hold it, as the washerwoman is annoyed by its slipping from the sloppy bench, and so keeps it in the tub of water; and therefore, a little wooden bowl should always be provided for it. A black bottle of ox-gall should also be kept in the laundry for use in washing colored muslins and percales, as it preserves their brightness. If its odor is disagreeable, add a little alcohol to it.

Coffee Starch.

This is excellent for starching dark clothing, and for men's linen coats and pantaloons, as it does not take out their color. Take two cups of boiling hot, strong coffee, made in the usual way, and add to it two table-spoonfuls of the best starch, mixed with enough cold water to make it a smooth, soft paste. While the coffee is boiling add the starch, stirring all the time. Let it boil for about quarter of an hour, and give it a stir round with a spermaceti candle. Turn it into a pan, and when nearly cool dip in the clothing to be starched. If too thick, thin it with warmish water.

To Wash Black Woolen Stockings.

Wash them in weak suds made of warmish water, to which is added a table-spoonful of ox-gall. Rinse till no color runs. Iron on the wrong side.

To Stiffen Linen.

To starch cuffs and collars that require to be very firm, boil the starch after mixing it with cold water, to a smooth consistency; and into a pint of starch drop a bit of white wax half the size of a hazel-nut, and stir in one tea-spoonful of alcohol, or spirits of wine. The effect of the spirit is to retain and increase the stiffness of the starch, while the wax prevents it from sticking to the flat-iron. When an iron sticks to the starch, rub bar soap over the bottom of it.

Linen collars, cuffs and shirt fronts should be first starched with boiled starch, and allowed to dry, and then, with a little starch dissolved in cold water, and be left an hour or so and then ironed. There is a great art in mixing starch, and if boiling water is used, it need not be boiled only a few moments. A little borax often gives linen a good gloss, if it is dissolved in the boiling water. Run starched clothes through the wringer to make the starch strike into every part of the linen.

To Bleach Lingerie Lace and Embroidery.

After washing and boiling it, let it lie all day in very strong blue-water, and at night lay it upon the grass. As it dries, wet it with soap and water. When white enough, boil or wash again. Many laundresses think that boiling has a tendency to yellow lace and linen, and only scald the fabric.

To Wash Black or White Prints.

It often happens that black percales or calico, which run a white pattern on a black ground, will not bear washing in the usual way, as the spots will become reddish, and the black ground dull. When the white clothes are all taken out of the boiler, put in the black print dress and let it boil up for ten minutes; then take it out and pour over it enough cold water to make it comfortable for the hands, and rub it thoroughly. Rinse in lukewarm water to take out the suds, and again in very blue-water. Starch in coffee starch, run it through the wringer, let it dry, dip it into cold water, wring it, and roll it in a towel for an hour or more. Then iron on the wrong side.

How to Iron.

Ironing requires patience and time; one cannot iron rapidly and do the work well. There are ironing machines with iron rollers, and mangles are often used for large articles, like sheets and table cloths, but for home use nothing has been found to equal the common flat-iron.

Cleanliness is a decided essential in the ironing-room, and soiled irons, with a greasy stove, can never give satisfaction, while wood fires which need frequent replenishings, are not as desirable as coke or coal. Kerosene stoves are now introduced, that supply every need to the laundress, and the "FLORENCE OIL STOVE" cannot be too highly recommended, not only in the laundry, on account of its model flat-heater, which does away with all heat in the kitchen, and can be used on the piazza or under the shade of trees, but also for all work in the kitchen, such as baking, broiling and boiling. Rightly managed, no smoke or smell of kerosene can be perceived.

Ironing blankets should be thick, and the ironing sheet clean and whole. For ironing embroideries, laces, etc., additional thicknesses of flannel are required, so that the raised portions of the patterns can be made to appear in good relief. Articles should be neither too damp nor too dry, so as to look wrinkled when ironed; and they should be hung in a dry, warm place to dry and stiffen. If hung in the wind, out of doors, all the starch will be blown out.

How to Wash Blankets.

Make a good suds with bar soap and water, comfortably warm to the hand, and then pour in spirits of ammonia, a table-spoonful at a time, until the suds smell strongly of the ammonia, and turn in two ounces of powdered borax dissolved in boiling water. Shake all the dust out of the blankets, and then rinse them up and down and squeeze lightly in the hands, but do not rub them; it is that motion which fulls the wool and felts it together. Do not rub any soap upon them, but dip them well in the water; then rinse in plain water, warm to the hand, not hot. By folding the blankets lengthwise in a long, narrow strip, they can be drawn through a wringer, but should never be wrung through the hands. Then shake thoroughly and hang out, drawing the edges and corners smoothly together. When thoroughly dry, fold smoothly and place the bosom board over, with one or two flat-irons to hold it down, and the next day they will be fresh and sweet. Select a bright, sunny day for washing blankets, and never hang them out in a rain or a drizzle.

Another Method of Washing Blankets.

Put two large tea-spoonfuls of borax, powdered, into a pint bowl of the best soft-soap, and mix it thoroughly with a tub half full of cold water. Put in a pair of blankets, and let them soak over night. Next day dip them up and down, and squeeze them, but do not rub them, for that thickens the wool. Draw them up and down with the stick used for boiling clothes, and when all the soil seems removed, squeeze them out of the suds, but do not wring them, and put into a tub of warmish water—water with the chill off—and with the stick draw them up and down. When the suds are beaten out, put into strong bluing water, and then squeeze out as much as possible. Run the blankets through a wringer, and hang upon the lines, taking care to pull the corners evenly together. As the water drips down into the edges, squeeze it out with the hands gently.

All flannels should be washed with lukewarm water, as boiling or hot water felts the wool and hardens the fabric. Blankets washed in this way will be always soft and fleecy, and last for years.

How to Wash Old Flannels.

When flannel has become yellowed by age, in order to whiten it, dissolve a pound and a half of soap in six gallons of water, and add to it one table-spoonful of spirits of ammonia. Place the flannel in the water, stir it rapidly around for a short time, and rinse it up and down, then take it out and rinse it in pure water.

To Wash Black and Blue Linens.

When black or navy blue linens and percales are to be washed, do not use soap, but wash and pare thinly three or four potatoes, and grate them into soft lukewarm water. Wash the linens in this, first adding a tea-spoonful of *aqua ammonia*. Rinse them in cold blue-water, made quite dark colored. They will need no starch, but should be dried and ironed on the wrong side.

To preserve the natural color of *ecru* and brown linens, boil a handful of hay in the water, and use wheat bran instead of soap.

To Do Up Lace Curtains.

After the curtains are taken down, shake and brush out all the loose dust, and then wash them at once in warm water (not hot) in which a little washing soda has been dissolved. Wash by squeezing in the hands and rinsing up and down in the suds. Lace cannot be rubbed on a board, or endure harsh treatment. If there are brown spots rub on a little hard soap. Blue the rinsing water, if you do not desire the now fashionable yellow hue. Make a thin starch, and stiffen it with a table-spoonful of powdered borax. Shake out the curtains very gently, as handling will lessen their stiffness. Lay sheets on the floor of an unoccupied room, and pin the curtains to them, at intervals of two or three inches. This pinning down process, however, is a very hard one for unsupple knees, and a pair of old quilting frames, with pegs and auger holes to vary according to the size of the curtain, will answer much better. Little tinned hooks or catches can be thickly placed along the inside of the frames, and the edge of the lace fastened to them, and five or six curtains can be thus dried at once, in the sun, in a short time, and they will look like new lace. Nottingham, or any other kind of lace, can be done up beautifully by this method.

To Remove Stains of Wine or Fruit From Table Linen.

Stains of claret wine can be removed by rubbing them while wet with common salt. Turn the contents of the salt cellar directly over the stain, and rub in the salt with the finger, until the redness disappears entirely.

A sure way of extracting fruit stains from table linen, is to tie up some cream of tartar in the stained part, so as to form a little bag, then put the linen into cold soap-suds, and let it boil awhile. Then wash and rinse well, dry and iron, and no stains will appear.

Another method is to mix in equal quantities, soft soap, slacked lime, and saleratus, and rub the stain with the preparation, and lay the linen in the sun, with the mixture plastered on. When it has lain two or three hours, rub it off; if the stain still appears, apply some more of the mixture. When it cannot be seen, wash out the linen at once, as it will decay the fabric.

To Restore Mildewed Linen.

Take soft soap and powdered chalk in equal quantities, and rub all over the discolorations. Spread the linen in the sun for an hour or so, then wash it off.

Hints Upon Soap Making.

Soap is one of the accessories of housekeeping, which adds greatly to the cleanliness of everything connected with it. And it has been said, with truth, that the amount of soap used by the inhabitants of a country, measure its grade of civilization, for habitual cleanliness of the home and the person is surely one of its greatest influences.

Chemically considered, soap is the union of fat, or oil, with an alkali, either potash or soda. The latter possesses the cleansing power, but if used alone, it would tend to destroy the substance; therefore, the need of oleaginous matter. In cities, the housekeeper can exchange her refuse fat for excellent soap, but in the country one is forced to manufacture it, and where wood is consumed for fuel, both the alkali and the fat are serviceable, and the ashes are still of some use in the garden.

Soap making, therefore, is one of the country arts, and in every village there are one or two women, who go from house to house in the early Spring, and the leach having been duly arranged a few days previously, attend strictly to their business, and never fail to produce good results.

The lye is first boiled in a large brass kettle, and the grease turned into it, and then boiled together until it is entirely mixed. The addition of a pound of resin in the lump, and a pound of borax, (put into the boiling kettle,) to each barrelful of soap, will improve it greatly for all cleansing operations, while it will prevent the soap from injuring the hands by the action of the lye, which, in newly made soap, is always troublesome. After the boiling soap is turned into the barrel, put in a pail of cold water, and stir it up with a stick, beating it for fifteen minutes. Add another pailful of weak lye, taking that which will run from the leach tubs at the last, by pouring in pailfuls of hot water. Alternate with a pailful of cold water, and one of weak lye, until the barrel is filled. Upon the amount of stirring the soap receives will depend its whiteness, and the resin and borax will make it look like a jelly.

Soft Soap Without Ashes.

Twenty pounds of white potash, and twenty pounds of clear grease, free from bones, will make thirty-two gallons of soap. Melt the grease, or, if preferred, put it into the barrel cold. Pour a pail of boiling water upon the potash, which will melt sooner if pounded fine. Stir it till dissolved, and turn it upon the grease. Mix a pound of borax in a pailful of boiling water, and turn upon the grease. Stir until it is all mixed together. Add cold water as directed in the recipe above.

To Make Hard Soap.

Take six pounds clear, hard grease, six pounds sal-soda, and three pounds of lime in the lump, with seventeen quarts of water. Turn the water over the lime and soda, in a kettle, and let them come to a boil, on the fire—then place the kettle away until the next day.

Put the grease in a kettle, and pour the clear lye over it, stopping as soon as the sediments mix with it. Boil it until it thickens like syrup, stirring constantly. Just before you take it off, throw in a large handful of kitchen salt (fine).

When it is dissolved turn the soap into a tub and stir it until it begins to harden somewhat. Then cut it into bars.

If you would like to make it very nice, add half a pound of powdered borax to the grease before the cold lye is poured on to it. This recipe will make excellent soap for all washing purposes; woolens, calicoes, etc., can all be cleaned with it without injury to the fabric.

To Make Pure White Soap.

Take twenty pounds of washing soda and put it in a barrel, with a few small lumps of quicklime upon it. Pour over it three gallons of boiling water, and let the lye leach out of holes made in the bottom of the barrel—having placed a layer of straw under the sal-soda, to act as a filter to the lye. To every gallon of this lye add eight pounds of clear, white grease, and boil it gently for three or four hours, or until it is completely saponified, which can easily be tested by putting a flat bladed knife into the boiling mass. If it adheres closely the soap has boiled long enough. Stir it frequently, and add a large handful of fine salt. Add half a pound of borax to each eight pounds of grease. Turn out into a wooden box and cut in bars, when sufficiently cool. It is excellent for all purposes.

Useful Soap for Scrubbing, etc.

Take two pounds of common yellow or white bar soap, shave it in very thin slices, and add to it two ounces of powdered borax, and two quarts of cold water; put it in a tin pail or in an earthen jar, and set it on the back of the stove until it is well dissolved; stirring it frequently. A very little heat is needed to make it liquid, and when thoroughly mixed together it can be taken from the fire, and when cooled it will be of the consistency of a thick jelly. A piece an inch square will make a lather for a gallon of water.

It is invaluable for scrubbing and cleaning floors, washing dishes, and for all household purposes.

An Excellent Shaving Soap.

Shave fine three pounds of the best white bar soap, add to it three-fourths of a pint of soft water, and one pound of palm oil. Melt it in an earthen bowl or tin pail, placed in a kettle of boiling water. Stir it well together; then add sixty drops of oil of lavender, and ten drops oil of neroli. These will perfume it deliciously. Stir well and turn it into a shallow pan of wood or tin, then cut it into squares as soon as it hardens sufficiently.

To Make Soap-Balls.

Shave thin two pounds of white bar soap into half a pint of boiling water. When melted add to it one pint of olive oil, half a pound of spermaceti, half an ounce of oil of almonds, half an ounce of powdered camphor, half a pint of rose water, a table-spoonful of alcohol, and twenty drops of essence of lavender. Stir it all together, let it boil ten minutes, pour it out into a tin basin until thick enough to roll up into hard balls, which must be done as quickly as possible. Stir in the essence after you have taken it from the fire, for it will lose its strength greatly if put in while boiling hot.

To Make Real Honey Soap.

Cut two pounds of common bar soap into thin shavings, and put it into a tin pail, with barely hot water enough to cover it. Place the pail into a kettle of boiling water, and when its contents are melted, stir them thoroughly, and add a quarter of a pound of honey and a quarter of a pound of almond oil, and a quarter of a pound of powdered borax. Mix all together by stirring well for ten minutes. Then add oil of cinnamon, a few drops, or oil of bergamot, or any scent which is preferred. Mix it well, and turn the soap into a deep dish to cool, then cut into squares. It can be used at once, but improves by age. It can be made into sand soap balls, by adding equal quantities of white sand and Indian meal, until it is so stiff that you can roll it in the hands. There is no soap that will whiten the hands like this.

How to Mend Broken China.

When a dish is broken do not let the pieces lie about where they will become soiled, but put them in a drawer, or mend them at once; for the best cements often refuse to hold because the parts united were not clean.

Make the layer of cement as thin as it can possibly be, and yet let it cover every particle of the edge, for a thin layer is stronger than a thick one. When the form of the pieces will admit of it, rub them together slightly before fixing in place, so as to cover every particle of space. Press very tightly together, and tie the parts together until the cement is dry. Those cements that are applied hot will harden the quickest, and it is a good plan to warm the pieces also.

Cracked crockery can be made strong by putting it into cold, skimmed sweet milk and letting it boil for an hour or more. Tie the parts together before you put them in, and let them remain so for a week, and they will last a great while.

A great deal can be saved by taking heed to these little things, and if you have not the time to do it, and can better afford to purchase new, give them to some poor neighbor who will be thankful for the opportunity to mend them, and add to her small store of crockery and glass.

Water-Proof Cement for Aquariums.

Take four ounces of glue, and two ounces of isinglass, put in a common glue or small kettle. Pour over them enough ale, or stale beer, to cover well. When it is well dissolved and mixed together, add one and a half ounces of boiled linseed oil, stirring it in by a few drops at a time. When cold, it looks like India rubber, and can be kept in a cake, and when needed, dissolved in a little boiling hot stale beer. It will mend furniture of all kinds, and is, also, excellent for joining bands for machinery, and to mend harnesses. But the cement must always be applied boiling hot, and allowed to dry thoroughly. By dipping a twist of tow into the cement, you can mend leaks in roofs, barrels, and the like.

Burgardien's Paste Glue.

M. Burgardien, of the Museum of Narbonne, has given his name to a cement of great value, which is, however, nothing more than silicate of potassa. It can be used to join or solder together various broken things, such as iron, blocks of stone, marble, or wood, of the largest size, or the most delicate fragments of glass, statuary, vases, mosaics, pottery, and furniture, in short, almost anything can be mended with its aid. With a small brush spread the silicate of liquid potassa over the surfaces to be joined, then press them together as closely as possible. After being held or fastened in this position for a short time, they will be firmly cemented, and we may strike them hard without separating them. Neither fire, water, nor cold, affects this artificial adhesion.

Lime and Egg Cement.

This is made by moistening the edges of broken glass or crockery ware, with the white of an egg, not beaten, and dusting on some lime from a little muslin bag filled with air slacked lime. Or a surer method is to slack a fresh bit of lime in a small quantity of boiling water. Then beat the white of an egg with a table-spoonful of water, and sift in enough lime to form a thin paste, which must be used at once, as it hardens quickly. This is a valuable cement as it resists heat and water.

White Lead for Mending Glass and Crockery.

White lead, such as comes in small tin boxes, is also excellent for mending all kinds of ware, excepting iron, tin and wood. Take it out with a match or a small splinter of wood, and smear both edges of the pieces, then join them firmly, and tie together with twine to hold the pieces firmly, until the lead hardens. It may take a week before it will be fit to use. A small bit of narrow white braid or tape, put on the outside or inside of the break, helps to hold it closer.

To Make Liquid Glue.

Dissolve one-quarter of a pound of gum-shellac in three ounces of naphtha. Put the shellac into a wide-mouthed bottle, and pour the naphtha upon it. Ask the druggist where you purchase the naphtha, to pour it in. Keep the bottle closely corked, but stir it up three or four times in the first forty-eight hours. When the shellac is thoroughly dissolved, the glue is ready for use, and it forms a very strong cement for all kinds of furniture.

Rice Flour Cement.

Mix four table-spoonfuls of rice flour with just enough cold water to make a thin batter. Simmer it gently over the stove, and it will form a durable and delicate cement for joining paper or card boxes as baskets, which now afford both employment and amusement to ladies.

If made thick as plaster, it can be formed into busts and models of all kinds, which, when thoroughly dry, can be polished highly, by rubbing with a piece of chamois leather.

Cement for Glasses, Etc.

Place in a large-mouthed bottle two ounces of isinglass, shredded finely, and two ounces of gum arabic powdered. Pour over them enough alcohol, of highest proof, to cover them. Put the cork in lightly, and place the bottle in a sauce-pan, and boil it until the gum and isinglass are entirely dissolved. Stir it from time to time with a little stick. Put a brush through the cork, and use for preparing microscopic objects, or for mending glass ware. It also makes an excellent mucilage.

How to Make a Fire and Water-Proof Cement.

Turn half a pint of vinegar into half a pint of milk. Let the curd form, and strain off the whey. Add to it the whites of five eggs, and beat it with an egg beater for ten minutes. Stir into it powdered quicklime, just slacked enough to powder fine, until it is a thick paste. Keep it tightly corked from the air. Broken dishes, etc., mended with this cement, will resist the action of both fire and water, and will rarely, if ever, separate in the same place.

Prepared Glue for Constant Use.

To any quantity of glue use common whiskey or alcohol instead of water. Put the bits of glue, well broken up, into a bottle; fill up with the spirit and set it in a closet or where it is warm for a week, then it will be ready to use without the application of heat.

Glue thus prepared will keep for years, and will be fit for use at all times, unless the weather is very cold, then place the bottle in boiling water for a few moments. To obviate the difficulty of the stopper becoming tight from the glue, it is a good plan to make the glue in a tin box, and the cover will fit on tightly without sticking. It must be closed tight or the spirit will evaporate.

To Make Mouth Glue.

This is made by dissolving pure glue with one quarter of its weight in coarse, brown sugar, and in as small a quantity of boiling water as possible. When it is perfectly liquid, turn it into a shallow tin pan, having oiled it a little with butter. As it stiffens, cut it into small squares. When required for use, moisten one end with the mouth. It will be found very convenient in a lady's work box or desk.

Little Things Worth Knowing—How to Rebake Stale Bread.

Soak a stale loaf of bread or some rolls in water for a moment or two, and then rebake for more than half an hour, and they will be in every respect equal to newly baked bread.

To Purify the House.

For purification of the air in stale rooms, mix one pound of the chloride of lime in eight gallons of water. Shake it before using, and throw a quart of it daily down the pipes in bathing-rooms and kitchens, and put dishes of it in the rooms.

To Preserve the Color of a Print Dress.

Wash in lukewarm water with a little hard soap, but make the suds before the dress is put in. Add one table-spoonful of borax and one of common salt to the lukewarm rinsing water. Wring tightly and roll up in a coarse towel or piece of a sheet, until dry enough to iron.

To Destroy Flies.

Boil the parings of potatoes in a little water for an hour, skim them out, and boil the water down to a few table-spoonfuls. Sweeten with molasses, and turn on to plates. It is a deadly poison. Another method is to boil quassia chips to a strong decoction, sweeten and proceed as above.

To Remove Egg Stains From Silver Spoons.

When eggs are eaten frequently the silver spoons become discolored because of the sulphur the eggs contain, which, uniting with the silver, form sulphurate. The quickest and the best way to remove the stain, is to rub the spoon with fine salt, between the thumb and finger, and then wash in soap-suds.

To Remove Freckles.

Take one ounce of lemon juice, a quarter of a drachm of powdered borax, and half a drachm of sugar. Mix and let them stand in a glass bottle for a few days, then rub it on the face and hands night and morning. Two table-spoonfuls of lemon juice would equal an ounce.

Hair Wash to Cleanse the Scalp.

Add six drops of *aqua ammonia* to a wine-glass of warm water, and with a small bit of sponge or flannel wash the head thoroughly, dividing the hair into partings, so that all the skin is wetted. This not only cleanses the scalp quickly, but also preserves the color of the hair. It can be applied once a week, before going to bed, with very good effect.

To Remove Pimples from the Face.

These unsightly excrescences arise from eating fat meats and other articles of food which produce indigestion; and it will require some little amount of self-denial at the table to remove them, and the sufferer should never indulge in late suppers, and should take as much outdoor exercise as possible. A small pinch of flour of sulphur dissolved in a gill of milk, and taken every morning, is an efficacious remedy, but it will take some little time to produce the desired effect. Keep your feet dry, and avoid the damp while taking the sulphur.

To Take Fresh Paint Out of a Coat.

Take a piece of broadcloth, and rub the wrong side of it on the paint; if no other cloth is at hand, part of the inside of the coat skirt will do. This simple application will usually remove paint that is quite fresh. If it has hardened rub it out with a little chloroform on a silk or woolen rag. This will also take paint out of the finest fabrics of silk or woolen.

To Wash Silk Stockings.

Take lukewarm water and add to it half a tea-spoonful of spirits of ammonia, or a small bit of carbonate of ammonia. Mix a little white bar soap with the water, and wash the stockings clean. Rinse them in lukewarm water made quite blue. Dry in a warm place quickly. Silk handkerchiefs can be washed in the same way.

To Bleach a Faded Dress.

Wash the dress in very hot, strong suds, and then boil it until the color has disappeared. Rinse it in bluing water, and dry in the sun. Should it not be quite white, let it lie in the sun, on the grass, for several days.

To Black a Brick Hearth.

Mix some black lead with a little soft soap and water, boil it, and put it on with a scrubbing brush. The soap affixes the lead.

How to Ventilate a Chamber.

For ventilation, open your windows both at top and bottom. The fresh air rushes in at the bottom, and the foul air makes its exit at the top. Thus you can let in a friend and expel an enemy.

To Repair Towels.

When chamber and kitchen towels are thin in the middle, cut them in two and sew the selvages together and hem the sides.

To Remove Grease Spots from Books.

Scrape some French chalk, or take some powdered whiting, and lay as much on the grease spot, both sides of the paper, as will cover it. Then press a moderately hot flat-iron on the spot, covering the powder with a small piece of blotting or common brown paper. The heat will dissolve the grease, and mix itself with the chalk. If it does not come out the first time repeat the process.

To Restore Plated Goods.

Moisten a little common whiting with some nitrate of silver, sufficiently to make a paste, and rub it on the worn places with a soft brush—polish with leather. You can have the articles electroplated at a moderate price.

To Wash Thread Lace.

Rip off the lace carefully, and pick out the loose bits of thread and roll it very smoothly and securely around a champagne or black glass bottle that has been closely covered with white linen. Fasten each end of the lace, and take care not to crumple or fold in any of the scallops or pearlings. If it is very yellow and soiled, wet the lace with a bit of sponge dipped into olive oil. Then cover it with a soft linen cloth wrapped around it. Fill the bottle with cold water, and put it into a small kettle filled with a strong lather of cold water and white soda soap. Let it stand upright in the suds, and boil for an hour or so. Drain off the suds and remove the coverings, and rinse the lace in cold water. Let it dry on the bottle, and when you take it off press it in a sheet of paper placed between the leaves of a large book.

How to Buy Gloves.

Nothing looks worse than shabby gloves, and as they are expensive articles of dress, they require a little management in purchasing. Do not wear a new pair to church in the evening; the warmth of the gas, etc., gives a moisture to the hands, and spoils them. Wear an old pair in wet weather, as drops of rain will injure them, and carrying an umbrella soils them. It is the poorest economy to buy cheap gloves, as they never wear well.

To Extract Grease Spots From Silk.

Lay the grease spot upon a thick sheet of blotting or brown paper; place another piece of the same paper over the spot, and press a moderately warm flat-iron over it for a minute or so, till the stain disappears. Rub the stained part with a bit of soft silk or flannel.

To Restore Crape.

When a drop of water falls on a black crape veil or dress, it leaves a white mark. To take it out, spread the crape on the table, laying a book upon it to hold it in place. Put an old piece of black silk underneath it, then dip a camel's hair pencil into the inkstand, and rub over the mark; gently wipe it dry at once with a bit of silk.

Sachet Powders for Perfuming Desks and Bureaus.

No. 1. Half an ounce of orris root powdered, four drops otto of rose, one and a half ounces of powdered starch.

No. 2. Two ounces of orris root powdered, ten drops of essence of ambergris, four drops of oil of neroli.

No. 3. Gum benzoin, half a drachm; musk, two grains; ambergris, four grains; storax, half a drachm; one ounce powdered cloves; half an ounce of powdered orange peel.

Mix each recipe separately, and put in cotton wool and keep in desk or bureau drawers.

To Extract Ink from Mahogany.

Dilute half a tea-spoonful of oil of vitriol with a large spoonful of water, and apply to the ink spot with a feather. Let it remain wet for a minute or so, and rub off quickly with a bit of old silk or flannel. If not removed repeat, but if allowed to remain too long, it will make a white spot.

To Remove Ink Stains.

Procure a two-ounce bottle, and put into it five cents' worth of oxalic acid, and fill it up with warm water. Put a bit of linen rag over the stain, and pour a few drops of it upon the cloth. It ought to take out the stain at once; if not, rub it gently with the dampened cloth. If there was logwood in the ink it will, however, leave a reddish stain, but rub it with a little chloride of lime dissolved in water, and it will disappear.

To Mend Sheets and Shirts.

In mending sheets and shirts, always put on pieces sufficiently large to cover not only the rent, but the thin spots surrounding it. If you neglect to do so, the first washing will show your mistake, as the thin parts will give way from the weight of the new cloth.

A Wire Fire-Guard.

A wire fire-guard for each fireplace costs but little, yet greatly diminishes the risks to life and property by fire.

To Polish Patent Leather Boots.

Mix a table-spoonful of sweet oil with a tea-spoonful of turpentine, and rub it over the boots with a bit of sponge; then polish with a soft rag. If there are any cracks in the leather, fill them up with common boot blacking before you use the sweet oil and turpentine. In fact, any furniture polish will do to polish this kind of leather, and it will render them more lasting, as well as give them a good polish.

To take a tight Ring from the Finger.

If the finger on which the ring is placed has become too large, or is swollen, pass a needle with some soft thread in the eye, under the ring, and pull one end of the cotton upwards with the hand, while you twist the remaining cotton around the finger several times, until it reaches the nail. Then pull on the other thread, and it is usually an easy matter to slide the ring off the finger, no matter how difficult it has been before the experiment was tried.

To Prevent Discolorations of the Skin after a Blow.

Take a little dry starch or arrow root, and merely moisten it with cold water, and lay it on the injured part. Do it at once, so as to prevent the air from touching the spot, and no sign of it will be seen. It can also be applied hours afterwards with decided effect, but will not prevent it wholly.

To Remove Grease Spots from Carpets, Table Cloths, Dresses and Furniture.

Heat the poker red-hot and hold it over the grease spot within an inch of the material. In a moment or two the grease will disappear. Be sure not to place the poker so near as to scorch the grease spot. It needs a steady hand to hold it, and, if possible, apply a hot flat-iron over several sheets of brown paper.

Polishing Paste for Tins and Britannia Ware and Brass.

Powder some rotten stone very fine. Mix it with some soft soap until it is a stiff paste. Add to half a pound of the paste two ounces of oil of turpentine. It can be made up in balls, and it will soon harden and keep any length of time. When using it, mix a small piece with water and rub over the articles with a woolen cloth; afterwards rub off with a dry cloth, and polish with newspapers. Wash all articles to be cleaned, first, with soap-suds, and apply the paste while damp.

To make Imitation Red, White or Black Coral Frames.

To every ounce of clear resin dissolved in a tin basin, add two drachms of English vermilion, well mixed together. Keep it in a liquid state over the fire, and dip into it little twigs and branches from which the bark has been peeled. Or dip in the small branches of the Norway pine and spruce. Or you can paint the branches all over with the composition. Then hold them over a gentle fire until all are smooth and even as if polished. In the same way white coral can be imitated, by adding white lead to the resin in the same proportion, and black coral by adding lamp-black.

A Wash to fix Pencil Drawings.

One part isinglass to fifty parts water; melt over the fire, and strain through muslin; apply by dipping the drawing into it, and pinning on the wall to dry. Another method is to dip the drawing into a pan of skimmed milk; take it by the corners and lift it out carefully, and place on a slanting surface to drain and dry. This will also affix chalk drawings. Still another method is to hold the drawing over the steam of the tea-kettle, and as it rolls up with the heat, reverse it and steam the back. Repeat this for two or three minutes. It can be washed afterwards with the thin size or the milk, and when nearly dry press it between two flat surfaces.

To Ventilate the Cellar and Keep Away Frost.

Whenever the temperature is above 32°, open the outside doors and let in a current of fresh air, and soon you will see the benefit of it in the increased health of your family, and in the purity of the air of the house, while your fruit and vegetables will keep better. It is a good plan to keep a thermometer in the cellar, and whenever it rises above 45°, open the doors and let them remain open an hour or so. Do this at noon time, when the air is warmest, and on a bright, sunny day. If there is a furnace in the cellar, it will need ventilating oftener, because its warmth consumes the air and makes it stale, and the doors can be left open from eleven to three o'clock, three or four times a week, if the outside air is not very cold. When there is danger of frost in a cellar, carry down several pails of hot water and sprinkle all over the floor just before retiring for the night, and, even if it forms into ice, there will be less danger of freezing fruit and vegetables, for water, in freezing, takes the frost out of the air. Often a cistern will freeze over, when potatoes will receive no injury.

How to Prepare Tracing Paper.

Tracing paper of the best quality can be made by painting over fine tissue paper with equal parts of oil of turpentine and mastic varnish. To make it, the tissue paper should be spread out perfectly flat on a level surface, and the liquid applied carefully over its surface with a soft brush. While doing this, care should be taken that every part of the paper should be completely covered, and that no more varnish is applied to one part of the paper than another. When the tissue paper is finished, hang it to dry on a string stretched across the room. During the drying, keep the room at a good heat, and perfectly free from dust. In a hot day, hang the paper out of doors in the sun. If it is desirable to paint in water-colors on the transparent paper, it can be brushed over with a solution of purified ox-gall.

How to Render Paper Transparent.

One part of castor-oil dissolved in two or three parts of spirits of wine, will make paper transparent, and as the spirit evaporates quickly, the paper will become fit for use in a short time. A drawing in pencil or India ink can thus be made, and if the paper is then placed in spirits of wine, the oil will disappear, and the paper become opaque.

Sympathetic Inks for Postal Cards.

If a weak solution of sulphuric acid (oil of vitriol) is used in writing, it will be invisible when dry, and will remain so until the card is held before the fire, when the letters will turn a brownish black and can be easily read. The reason is, that diluted oil of vitriol has no action on paper, but when exposed to heat some of the water is driven out, and the acid at once chars the paper. Another way is to write with a colorless solution of sulphate of iron (green copperas), or sulphate of copper (blue copperas). When dry, this writing will also be invisible, but if dipped into a solution of prussiate of potash it can be read easily. In the case of the iron the writing will present a blue tint; in that of the copper a brown. Another method consists in writing with a colorless solution of the nitrate of lead; when dry, nothing can be seen on the card, but if it is exposed to the vapor of hyposulphate of ammonia, the lines will at once turn a deep black, because of the formation of sulphuret of lead.

A Use for Old Corks.

Old corks are usually considered useless, but a proposal has been made that they should be preserved and sent to some central place, where they could be made useful in manufacturing cork belts, jackets, and the like, for saving life in shipwrecks. The corks could be sewn into some water-proof cloth, and really made of essential service. Those of our readers who contemplate a sea voyage,

HOUSEHOLD HINTS AND RECIPES.

can avail themselves of the hint, and manufacture life-buoys by quilting corks into cloth, and sewing on strings to attach it to the body.

To Disinfect Clothing by Sulphur.

To disinfect clothing, sponge or sprinkle it lightly with water and milk of sulphur, in the proportion of a tea-spoonful to a pint of water, and then iron it with a flat-iron hot enough to volatilize the sulphur, without scorching the clothing.

Sponge Boot Blacking.

Mix a quarter of a pound of ivory-black with half an ounce of oil of vitriol, and a table-spoonful of sweet oil. Stir up smoothly, then add half a pint of molasses; stir it well, and thin out slowly with three pints, or two quarts of vinegar, according to proper thickness for applying with a sponge.

A Preparation for Removing Grease Spots, etc.

Scrape fine a quantity of dry, white, bar soap, and cover it with sufficient alcohol to dissolve it. Then add the yolk of an egg, and stir it into a paste. Add to this a little turpentine, and also enough fuller's earth to make a thick paste. Put it into a wide-mouthed vessel, and keep it tightly covered. When required for use, moisten the spot with warm water, and rub in the paste with a bit of flannel. When it is dry, brush it off. This will extract all stains but those caused by ink or rust.

An Ink for Marking Linen with Stencil Plate.

Take two parts of sulphate of manganese and mix it with four parts of white powdered sugar, and one part of lamp-black. When it is well mixed, add enough water—drop by drop—to make it partly liquid. When required for use, spread the paste on a piece of thick cloth, and press the metal stamp upon it gently, so as to receive a thin coating of ink, then stamp the fabric.

When a stencil plate is used, pass the ink over it with a stiff brush. After the ink is applied to the linen, let it dry, and then moisten it with a very weak solution of caustic potash, by which the soluble sulphate of manganese is decomposed in the pores of the linen, into the insoluble black oxide of manganese, which is very durable.

To Polish Furniture.

Rub the furniture thoroughly with a soft flannel or leather, and then polish it with the following mixture, using a very little of it at once on a flannel: Mix thoroughly a quarter of a pint of turpentine, a quarter of a pint each of linseed oil, and the same measure of alcohol and vinegar. Shake up well in a bottle; rub the furniture briskly, and polish with a silk handkerchief.

Care of Woolen Curtains.

Winter curtains that are to be laid aside during the Summer months, should be shaken and well brushed, then folded neatly and put away with dry bran spread between the folds. This will make them look bright and fresh when taken out; but fasten the boxes securely, so that mice will not be attracted by the bran.

All woolen goods should have lumps of camphor, or better still, chips of cedar wood, or of Russia leather, put into the boxes with them, to exclude the moths.

How to Remove Mildew.

Make a very weak solution of chloride of lime, a heaped up tea-spoonful to a quart of water; strain it carefully, and dip the spot on the garment into it, and if the spots do not disappear, lay it in the sun for a few minutes. If they are still visible, dip it again into the lime water. Rinse the cloth in clear water, as soon as the spots are out. This will not wear the fabric.

Care of Pictures.

Oil pictures require an occasional dusting and polishing, but it is an operation that demands great care. If done with a feather brush, it is not always well accomplished, and a pad of cotton-wool will often be found to produce the best effect, but the operator must not bear with any force upon the canvas, lest she should produce minute cracks that will spoil the picture.

They should, also, be carefully polished once in awhile, and the best way is to breathe gently upon the surface, and rub it lightly off.

Or a little roll of cotton-wool can be dipped in lukewarm water and squeezed as dry as possible, and delicately wiped over the picture, drying it at once with a bit of chamois skin.

A piece of sponge, if not used too wet, will also remove smoke and fly specks. It is always better to return to such small spots a second time, than to leave them wetted too long.

Cold tea will clean varnished pictures so as to make them look fresh and bright. Rub the colors dry with the chamois skin, but touch them very lightly, else you will do more harm than good.

To Stain Woods.

Burnt umber will give a black walnut color, and burnt sienna a mahogany hue. Purchase them in powder, and put it in a tin pail, or a common jar, and stir it up to a thick liquid paint, with stale beer or ale. Water will do, but ale does not dry in so quickly, and admits of more rubbing in, and as the harder it is rubbed in the better will be the stain, the former is more desirable. Put it on with a paint brush, or if that is not come-at-able, rub it on with a bit of flannel. If you desire to stain a set of shelves or a cupboard, select the color, prepare it, and rub in the stain. Do it evenly, rubbing all one way, and with long strokes, up and down, not cris-cross. Let it dry in thoroughly, then varnish with shellac varnish, made by dissolving half a pound of shellac in strong alcohol. Put the shellac into a glass jar, cover it with alcohol, and set it in a warm place. When melted, if it is too thick to spread easily from the brush, add more alcohol. With a varnish brush put it on the wood work; let it dry in perfectly. Add another coat, and before it is dry, only hardened a little, rub it dry with a bit of woolen dipped in sweet oil, and you will be surprised at the hard, smooth finish you will have produced.

To Cleanse Hair or Clothes Brushes.

Dissolve a piece of washing soda about the size of a walnut with an atom of soap, in a basin quite full of warm water. Pass the hairs of the brush through the surface of the water, taking care not to wet the handle or the back of the brush, as it not only spoils the varnish, but loosens the fastenings. Shake out the brushes several times from the water, and they will be white and clean.

Another method is to wet the brushes a little, and then scatter saleratus over the bristles, and taking a brush in each hand, rub them smartly together for a few minutes. Then wash in clear water, only on the surface, but rub the brushes together again. Dry in the sun, and they will be as good as new.

To Clean Doeskin Riding Gloves.

Wash them in a little soap and water to remove the soil, and then pull them into shape; but be careful not to wring them in the washing, as that shrinks the leather. Then lay them on the table, well pulled into shape, and rub them with a dye made of powdered yellow ochre, and pipe clay, mixed into a paste with vinegar or stale beer.

If the gloves are dark colored, use a mixture of fuller's earth and rotten stone, moistened in the same way. When the gloves are half dried they must be rubbed with a soft cloth, and stretched by the hands to make them soft and pliable, or they will become too stiff and tear easily.

When perfectly dry, beat them with a stick to remove all traces of the powder, and then place a sheet of paper over them, and press them flat with a warm iron, and they will look fresh and new. The iron must not be hot, but only warm enough to press into a good shape.

To Clean White Kid Gloves.

Stretch them on a board, and rub the soiled spots with powdered magnesia or cream of tartar. Let them lie in it an hour, and rub them over with a little powdered alum and fuller's earth mixed together. Leave them for an hour or so, then brush it all off, and dip a flannel in finely powdered whiting and polish the gloves thoroughly.

Another method is to take a little sweet milk, and a cake of white soap, and a soft napkin. Moisten a small spot of the latter with the milk, rub it on the soap, then scour off the spots on the glove. If put on to the hand it can be done easier. As it dries, pull it white. This can be used to clean all kinds of tinted gloves as well as white kid gloves.

To Restore Black Kid Gloves.

Mix a little sweet oil with two or three drops of ink. Take a bit of black silk, and rub it over all the worn and white spots in the gloves. It will also restore black kid boots, when badly defaced.

To Clean Wash-leather Gloves.

First take out the grease spots with magnesia or cream of tartar. Then wash and squeeze them through a lather of white soap and lukewarm water; hot water will shrink them too much. Rinse first in lukewarm and then in cold water, and stretch into shape carefully; then hang in the sun or a warm place to dry.

Another way is to first remove the soiled spots, and then put on a glove and rub it with a clean sponge wetted in lukewarm soap-suds. Rinse them off, and rub with the sponge wetted in cold water. When almost dry put them on the hands until wholly so, and it will prevent them from shrinking and becoming too small for use.

Management of Earthen Ware.

New earthen ware should be soaked in cold water twenty-four hours before it is used, as it will then be less liable to crack. A good-sized wooden tub or bowl is the best for washing articles which are not greasy, such as tea-cups, etc. A small mop is indispensable to wash out the insides of pitchers and the like. A little sal-soda added to the water will cleanse jugs and pitchers, or cups that become stained, but it should be used very sparingly, and not often. A little milk added to the water will cleanse gilded and painted china better than soap, that is apt to take of the gilding. For tea cloths, those of soft linen are the most desirable; cotton fabrics are not sufficiently absorbent to dry earthen ware.

For washing greasy dishes, a tin pan with a partition in the center is most suitable, as one part of it can hold soap-suds, and the other clear water for rinsing the dishes. Dry, closet shelves, or those with glass doors are the best for keeping all kinds of earthen ware.

HOUSEHOLD HINTS AND RECIPES.

How to Sleep.

No perfect rest or sleep can be obtained with the mouth open, and as it is the great physician and restorer of mankind, it is essential for parents to educate their children to keep the lips closed, either waking or sleeping, excepting when speaking, etc.

"Contrast," says Mr. Catlin, in his book entitled, *Shut Your Mouth and Save Your Life*, "the natural repose of the Indian child, educated to keep its lips closed, with the uncomfortable slumbers of the infant of civilization, with its little mouth open." The savage mother never fails to press the lips of her infant together till she has fixed a habit that will last through life. The nostrils are evidently made for breathing; they form the natural outlet of the lungs. The sides of their air-passages are lined with hairs, which in some degree, at least, prevent the ingress of noxious matters in the air we breathe. And it is confidently stated that miasmas are prevented from entering the blood if one breathes only through them.

Therefore keep your mouth shut when you sleep, when you listen, when you are walking or running, and by all means when you are angry. The habit is difficult to acquire, but it is worth taking trouble to do so.

How to Lend and Borrow Books.

It is not unusual for persons to borrow books, and keep them such a length of time, that at last they really forget they are in their possession, or else forget to whom they belong. And sometimes even go so far as to imagine, and even state that they are their own property.

Such conduct is very annoying to lovers of books, who are also lovers of their neighbors, and desire to share with them the books they possess, so far as allowing them to read them; but also desire that they should be returned in good season and good order. And a careful person will never be guilty of such a decided breach of good conduct, but will keep a list of borrowed books, and see that they are duly returned to their respective owners. It is a good plan to keep all borrowed books upon a shelf, apart from other books, and placed in a conspicuous part of the house, so that they will constantly remind you of your derelictions.

There is no excuse for such peccadillos, and they often result in making book owners declare that not another book shall be lent out of the house. Or else they adopt the plan of keeping an account of all books lent, and to whom, and if the borrower should forget to return it, the lender can apply for it. This involves some trouble, but it is better than niggardly refusing to lend books to one's friends.

A Sure Indication of Death.

We read occasionally, startling accounts of apparent death, sometimes followed by burying alive, so it may not be unwise to give our readers the following method of determining the condition of the body. A medical gentleman states that if a drop of strong spirits of ammonia be injected beneath the skin, a red spot will surely appear should the patient be in a comatose state, but if death is actually present, no such effect can possibly follow.

Economy in Coals.

It is usual in many families to lay in a stock of coke as well as coal, and by having it broken up very small and mixed with the coal, the fire can be lighted much easier.

You can also produce a decided saving in your coal bills by mixing the ashes with coal-dust and small coal, and wetting it a very little; then put it at the back of the grate, and fill the front up with coal, and it will all burn together brightly and clear.

How to Wash Colored Silk Handkerchiefs.

Make a good suds in lukewarm water, in which a little bit of carbonate of ammonia has been dissolved; rub the handkerchiefs lightly in the hands till all the spots have disappeared. Then rinse them in lukewarm water, and squeeze them as dry as possible. Take hold of two corners and shake and snap each one for a few minutes. Roll in a soft towel, tightly, laying the handkerchief flat on the towel at first, squeeze tightly, and iron at once. Another method is to put three cents' worth of sugar of lead into the suds and proceed as above.

To Restore French Gold Ornaments.

Drop ten drops of spirits of ammonia into half a pint of water, and rub the ornaments with a soft brush. Dry in a napkin, and polish with chamois skin.

Woolen Wristlets.

When the season is very severe, a pair of wool knitted wristlets are of the greatest service in keeping the whole body warm; and we would especially recommend them to the aged and the delicate of both sexes, and also for little children.

The blood which flows through the arteries comes very near the surface at the wrists, as you can easily perceive by feeling your pulse. Keep it warm there, and the whole system is favorably affected. In the same way in cases of fever, the blood can be perceptibly cooled by rubbing the wrists with cologne or camphorated spirits.

The wristlets can be made three or four inches in length, and either crocheted or knitted round and round, and can be finished at the hand with a dainty ruffle. It is better to have two or three pairs, and change them frequently, as they soil easily. A pair of white woolen wristlets can be worn under the linen cuff or the frill, and not be perceptible.

To Restore Faded Black Alpacas and Cashmeres.

If you do not wish to rip the breadths apart, brush the skirts perfectly free from dust, and then sponge them on the right side with clear cold coffee, and iron with a moderately hot iron, on the wrong side—or over a bit of print, such as an apron. White goods will lint it. To restore a dress that is turned brown, cut the seams open close to the sewing—to save the time of ripping, and brush them free from dust.

Then take two spoonfuls of the extract of logwood, and two spoonfuls of the crystals of copperas, and put them into three or four gallons of boiling hot suds. Put in all the pieces of black goods you desire to color over, and let them boil five minutes. Take out and rinse in warm water, with a stick lifting them up and down. Do this thoroughly. Run through a wringer—and hang in the sun to dry; iron on the wrong side before they become too dry.

To Restore Faded Drab and Slate Colors.

Save the tea leaves and cold tea, for a few days, then boil in some water, and strain from the leaves, and treat as described above.

To Clean White Spar Ornaments.

Wash with "*Javelle Water*," rinse in plain water, wipe with a soft towel, and dry in the sun.

How to Build a Cistern.

A cistern can be built that will last a hundred years or more—and supply a large family with wholesome water for cooking and drinking purposes, and soft water for washing. Select a location near the house, (generally in the grass plat,) and for a cistern twelve feet in diameter in the clear, and ten feet deep from the bottom to the arch, dig a circular hole about fifteen feet in diameter, and from sixteen to seventeen feet in depth. See that the foundation is firm, and that the bottom is made level and smooth. Then cover it with one and a quarter inch boards, two thicknesses, laid cross-ways of each other. On these place two layers of sound, hard-burned paving bricks, with strong water lime cement. Then, leaving twelve feet space in the clear, build the outside circular wall, eight inches thick, of the bricks, raising it ten feet high; now commence turning the arch with a proper curve, and leave a hole in the top, two feet in diameter, to receive the cast iron curb. This and the cover being about three feet high, they should just reach the top of the yard or grass plat. Also build a partition wall, eight inches thick across the center of the cistern, and up to a little above the spring of the arch, leaving eight or ten bricks out of the bottom course, so as to let the water pass from one side of the cistern to the other; also build two low partitions, one each side of the center partition, each about two feet in the clear from the center partition, and two feet high, to hold the filtering material. All the walls must be laid in water lime cement, so that no water can get through from the outside; and the entire inside should be well plastered with Roman cement, to prevent the water tasting of the lime. The tops of the inside walls should be capped with clean flat stones.

Filtered Water.

The best of water loses nothing by filtration, and no house should be without a filtering fountain to be used when the water is muddy. An economical one can be made by taking out the head of a cask—setting it upright, and at a distance of about one-third from the bottom of it place a shelf or partition, pierced with small holes. On this shelf place a layer of clean, small pebbles, over it a quantity of animal charcoal made by burning bones, or else wood charcoal. Then scatter on an inch of fine sand, and another layer of pebbles. Over this put another partition with fine holes, or an iron strainer to prevent the water from disturbing the bed of pebbles, charcoal and sand. At the bottom of the cask, put in a cock to draw off the water. A pipe can come from the eaves to the cask, then a cover should be fitted in.

Burns and Scalds.

Cold water is the surest, most abundant, and the readiest remedy for burns or scalds that can be procured. Use it instantly, and it will prevent the skin from blistering, and remove the pain and smart. If possible immerse the burn in the water, holding it there for half an hour or more, or until all sensation of pain is relieved. If the part cannot be thus treated, dip thick cloths in water, and keep them wetted upon the burn all the time. Do not remove the cloth to let the air touch the skin, but wet them by dripping from a sponge. Keep outer cloths to catch the drops, and not dampen the clothing.

Antidotes to Poisons.

When you have swallowed a poisonous substance, and medical aid is not at once obtainable, take a cupful of warm water, in which a tea-spoonful of dry mustard has been mixed. If you have not dry mustard in the pantry, the china-closet will usually contain a mustard pot, and a tea-spoonful of its contents, mixed with the water, will very quickly produce nausea, and relieve you from all danger. Warm water alone will often prove efficacious—and if neither it nor the mustard are obtainable, a spoonful of powdered alum, stirred up in molasses, will produce the desired effect as speedily. Be sure however to keep these two articles, viz.: mustard and alum on the shelves of the pantry.

Remedy for Poison from Ivy.

This painful poison will yield quickly to a solution of sugar of lead. Dissolve a piece about the size of a hazel-nut in half a tea-cup of boiling milk, and apply it as hot as the sufferer can bear it, with a soft linen cloth. Three or four applications will usually effect a cure. If the poison is on the face, and is approaching the eyes or mouth, lay cloths wetted in the solution upon the face, covering them with dry cloths, and keep them damped all the time.

It is a marvelous antidote, and by watching attentively you can see the fevered blisters turn from white to yellow, while applying it; and its use will prevent a great deal of suffering. It is a good plan to make a solution of the sugar of lead in water, and keep it bottled, if one poisons easily by this noxious plant. Milk is more soothing than the water, but the latter can be applied as soon as the fingers or face begin to sting, and prevent the formation of the blisters at once.

How to Store Fruit for Winter Use.

When you are so fortunate as to have plenty of fruit, it is well to take some care of it, so that when the dark, damp days of November come, the waste of it will not be apparent. It should be carefully gathered and sorted, leaving all that is bruised and over ripe for immediate consumption, and to give away.

Then have a suitable room in which to keep it, a dry upper chamber that is dark, cool, and well aired, is just the place for it; and if rows of shelves are placed in it, apples and pears and grapes can be laid upon them, so as not to touch each other, and they will keep in good condition for months, if the room is frost proof.

The usual way of pouring out apples and pears, like grain, in the corners of cellars and store-rooms, and letting them ferment, and send forth obnoxious odors, is anything but cleanly. Far better to give away or sell at a low price, what is not needed for family use. Apples can be stored in a dry, cool cellar, and kept tightly covered after they have ceased to become damp. If grapes are packed in dry sawdust, after they have lain on shelves for a week or two, they will keep until into the spring.

To Make Boots and Shoes Water-Proof.

A good composition to make boots, etc., proof against snow and wet, can be made out of one part mutton suet, and one part beeswax, melted and well stirred together.

It should be applied at night hot; and in the morning wipe off the boots with a colored piece of flannel. Although when the composition is first put on, the leather will not polish as well as usual when blacked, yet after a few times it will take a brilliant polish. Another method of rendering leather water-proof and durable, is to dissolve half an ounce of Burgundy pitch in half a pint of drying oil, mixed with half an ounce of turpentine. Warm the boots slightly before the fire, and apply the mixture with a soft brush; a small paint brush is good for this purpose. Let them dry well, and then give them a second coat. Let the boots stand in a dry place for two or three days, and they will be ready for use; and will last much longer than if the leather had not been varnished with it.

How to Mend Old Boots and Shoes.

No matter how full of holes the soles may be, if the upper leathers are sound and the stitching firm, they can be covered with gutta-percha, and with a little expense they will be "Amaist as gude as new."

The gutta-percha can be bought in thin sheets, and a pattern taken of the sole and then cut out by it. Warm the soles a little, and press the gutta-percha firmly over them. Let them stand awhile, and they will do you good service.

On the other hand, if the tops of your shoes or slippers are shabby, and the soles perfectly good, they can be covered tightly with woolen cloth or velvet, stitched on as closely as possible to the regular seam. A pair of boots can be covered with black lasting so neatly, that one would easily mistake them for new boots.

A pair of slippers that are worn out can be made to do duty for sickness, if covered with knitting or crochet work, and be soft and warm to the feet.

How to Light Fires on Damp Mornings.

All housekeepers have some time realized the difficulty of lighting a fire in a still, damp morning, when the chimney will not draw, and vigorous blowing proves quite ineffectual to produce a flame.

Science explains the trouble as "caused by the difficulty encountered in overcoming the inertia of the long column of air in the pipe or chimney, by the small column of air that can be forced through the interstices of wood or coal, at the bottom of which the kindlings are lighted."

This may be remedied by first lighting a few bits of shavings or paper, upon the top of the coal or wood; thus by the heated air forcing itself into the chimney, an upward current is established, and the room is kept free from the gas or smoke which is so apt to fill it, while the fire will also light quickly, and burn brightly.

To Make Instantaneous Fire-Lighters.

One of the latest proposals has been to light fires by electricity, so that the fires in a house being laid ready over night, no one need stir out of bed till every room was comfortably heated. Even with electricity, however, fire-lighters of some sort would be indispensable, and we have heard of a new method that has recently been invented for making them out of a cheap and easily obtained material.

Turf or peat is cut into cakes about three inches in length, by three in width, and one inch in thickness.

It is then dipped first into mineral or vegetable oil, and then into pitch, tar or turpentine, and the result is a highly inflammable fire-lighter. These pieces should be thoroughly dried, and carefully stored away.

To Extinguish Fire in Chimneys.

There are several better ways to extinguish fires in chimneys, and either of them are better than the old-fashioned way of throwing water down them from the top, as it always damages the carpets, and often the furniture. One of the simplest methods is to throw handfuls of flour of sulphur over the dullest part of the burning coals, thus causing mephitic vapors to rise, which will extinguish the flames. Meanwhile shut up the doors and the windows of the room, thus decreasing the draught; and hold a piece of wet carpet or blanket so as to close up the mouth of the fire, after throwing on the sulphur. Then if the draught below is stopped, the burning soot will soon be extinguished for want of air.

If every fire-place were provided with a damper or shutter of sheet-iron or tin plate, large enough to fill it up entirely, fires in chimneys would rarely do any damage, as one need only apply the damper to put them out at once.

To Make a Storm-Glass.

Take two drachms of powdered camphor; half a drachm of pure nitrate of potash, and half a drachm of muriate of ammonia, both finely powdered by a druggist. Put these ingredients into a small glass bottle about ten inches in length, and one inch in diameter. A bottle that has held Farina Cologne answers the purpose exactly. Fill it with the strongest proof alcohol, half way up, then turn in boiled rain water cold, until it is within an inch and a half of the neck. Cork the bottle, not very tightly, and hang it in the shade near a window. The sun's rays injure it. If the weather promises fair, the upper part of the bottle is clear and transparent. If rain or snow threaten, the compound at the bottom rises slowly, and feathery particles float about the bottle.

Twenty-four hours before a storm, or a tempest, the substance will be partly on the surface of the liquid, seemingly like a leaf or spray, and the whole contents will be in a state of fermentation.

A Cheap Weather Glass.

Take a wide mouthed glass fruit jar, and fill it to within two or three inches of the brim with soft water. Turn a clean oil flask, such as olive oil comes in, with its neck within the fruit jar. Should the weather hold fair, the water in the neck of the flask will remain about half an inch above the level, but if rain or snow be near, the water will rise gradually in the neck; and if the atmosphere be very heavy, it will sometimes rise as much as two or three inches in a few hours.

The water does not need to be changed; and outdoors or indoors are alike immaterial, excepting in freezing weather, for if the water should freeze it would break the jar.

This simple apparatus will not indicate the exact amount of moisture in the atmosphere; but the warning given by the rise of the water in the neck of the flask, will often prevent the family wash from being wetted; and also disappointment in other domestic affairs, when a dry day is essential to the work.

To Renovate a Black Cloth Coat.

Boil half a pound of logwood, and a few bits of copperas in three pints of water until reduced to a quart. When cold strain it through a cloth, and add a half a wine-glass of spirits of wine; shake it well together. Brush the coat thoroughly, shaking out all the dust; then with a nail brush apply the mixture to all the soiled parts, hang up to dry in a warm place, then brush out well with a soft brush. If the coat collar is much soiled, clean it with inodorous Benzine, or with a bit of silk dipped in chloroform. Or grate a potato into a saucerful of water, and let it settle, then rub the collar with the potato water. Cold tea is also an excellent thing to clean soiled coats.

To Clean Plaster Figures.

Dissolve a small amount of whiting in just enough water to make a paste, and put it over the figure with a brush. A little isinglass or glue dissolved in the water before the whiting is added, will prevent its rubbing off.

To Clean Smoky Lamp Chimneys.

Put a tea-spoon of oil of vitriol into a little water, and dip pieces of newspaper into it and rub off the spots with them. Draw pieces of paper through the chimneys to wipe them dry.

To Restore Woolen Furniture Coverings.

Beat the dust out as clean as possible, then rub them over with a soft cloth, to remove all loose dust. Make a good lather of Castile or hard bar-soap, and dip a soft flannel into it, and wash out every part of the covering. Then rinse it off with a cloth dipped into a strong solution of alum and water. Thus prepared, not a moth-miller will touch it.

To Take Fruit Stains out of Linen.

Moisten the spot slightly with clear water, and then light several brimstone matches, and hold the spot over them, so that the sulphurous gas can reach the stain, and the spots will soon disappear.

To Take Iron Rust out of Linen.

Hold the part that is spotted with iron rust, over the top of a bowl filled with boiling water, and rub it out with lemon juice and salt, or with a solution of oxalic acid. When the spot disappears, wash out the place in boiling water.

A Plea for Ashes.

The hearth stone is fireless in many families, because the mistress of the household thinks it such an addition to the daily work, and also that it adds so much more to the dust and soil of the room. And, if after dint of persuasion and entreaty, a fire is allowed to cast its delicious warmth, and its healthful glow about the room; no sooner is it extinguished than her love of neatness banishes every ash and brand as if they were signs of disorder instead of comfort. Now we insist that ashes are clean,—so clean as to be used in cleansing paint, etc., and fire is the emblem of purity; so that a liberal pile of ashes does not denote a slatternly housewife—but on the contrary it protects the chimney back from injury, and also the hearth, and preserves embers and coal from being consumed too quickly, and it also preserves the coals for another day's use. So let us make the hearth as clean as we please, but let the ashes pile up on all sides as a safeguard, and a surety of warmth.

The Arrangement of Apartments.

The best way to arrange apartments to give them expression is to study light and shade, and the combination of drapery, furniture, and pictures. Then let the whole atmosphere breathe sociability and comfort, and do not give them an isolated air.

See how a room looks after a number of people have left it, and then as you set things to rights, let the chairs and ottomans remain as they were when the room was filled with guests.

Make little studies of these things, and you will give some character to your rooms, and not make them look as though a funeral was in preparation.

As you enter some rooms the chilling atmosphere is felt at once, and almost unconsciously to yourself, you put on a stiff, set demeanor. company manners, as they are sometimes styled; and you cannot even maintain a cheerful, gay spirit, while making a morning call.

Socrates' Advice on House Building.

Pray ought not he who cares to have a house built as it should be, contrive so that it should be as pleasant and convenient as possible to live in? Is it not then pleasant for it to be cool in Summer and warm in Winter?

Does not the sun, in such houses as front the south, shine obliquely, during the Winter time, into the porticoes, while in Summer it passes vertically over the roofs, and affords no shade? Is it not well, therefore, if at any rate this position for a house be a good one, to build it in such a way that it shall be the highest toward the south, so that the Winter sun may not be shut out, and lower toward the north, so that the cold winds may not beat upon it so violently?

To speak as concisely as possible, that would be probably the pleasantest and most beautiful dwelling-house to which the owner could most agreeably betake himself at all seasons, and in which he could most safely deposit his goods.

To Make a Rag Rug.

As the making of floor mats and rugs is much in vogue of late, various methods have been invented for using up old dresses, coats, vests and the like, in their manufacture. The following directions will produce quite a pretty rug, and also, one that will last for years.

Cut and sew the rags in the same way as for making a rag carpet, winding each color into balls by itself. Then with a large crochet hook, make diamonds about an eighth of a yard in length. Begin with one stitch, and make a stitch every time across until the center is large enough, then narrow one stitch every time until one remains. Draw the cloth firmly through this twice, and it will need no other fastening. Crochet two rows with black around the outer edge of each diamond. Crochet the pieces together with very strong yarn, by placing the points together and crocheting through each stitch. Put the colors together tastefully, and crochet three rows of black around the entire rug.

How to Use Kerosene Lamps.

Although the introduction of lamps for burning mineral oils is of comparatively recent date—the oil wells not being discovered at Oil Creek, Penn., until 1859—yet they have become so universally adopted, as to be considered almost a necessity in every house; for, even when gas is used, one or more kerosene lamps are usually at hand.

In the minds of many, however, the fear of a dangerous explosion is so great, that many careful housewives prefer to use candles for carrying about the house.

That these lamps are dangerous, if improperly used, no one doubts; but, if only ordinary care is exercised, there need be no more danger from them, than in the use of sperm oil, or common candles.

Mineral oil, although accounted as a recent discovery, was known to the ancients, and Pliny mentions the petroleum of Agrigentim, in Sicily, which was used in lamps under the title of "Sicilian oil."

For a few moments after a lamp is lighted, the flame should be kept low, as it will increase in size and intensity as the heat increases; while, if fully turned up on its first ignition, it will become too strong, and either break the chimney, or throw up smoke and soot. Besides this, the glass chimney should become gradually heated, or it is very likely to break.

It frequently happens that those who are inexperienced in the use of these lamps, make the mistake of turning the wick up until it stands just above the dome. To be sure, the lamp will continue to burn even when thus arranged, but its light will be feeble, and a most offensive odor is produced, because the combustion of the oil is not complete. On the other hand, if a lamp is turned down too low, the same escape of gas takes place. It is of the utmost importance to keep the perforated plate clean, and free from pieces of burnt wick, which are so liable to choke up the apertures and impede the progress of the air, which feeds the flame.

When the lamp is in good order, there will be no smell whatever, and, if any offensive vapor is given off, it should be regarded as sure evidence of imperfect combustion, which can always be traced to a deficiency of air, through the partial stopping of some of the apertures through which it is intended to pass.

In order to ensure perfect safety in the use of these lamps, the upper portion should be removed daily, and a little boiling water be poured through the holes. Then, the wick should completely fill the tube, in order to prevent any possibility of direct communication between the flame and the oil in the reservoir; and the lamp must never be filled while the wick is ignited. It is, also, essential to safety that the lamps should be filled every day, for, if the oil runs low in the lamp, an explosive gas will form upon its surface, and it is liable, if stirred, to explode; hence many of the accidents from the use of kerosene.

And lastly, but not least, on no account should the lamp be placed where the oil becomes much heated, for, if it is, an explosion is well-nigh certain. Cooks will sometimes place a lamp on a range, or on the boiler of a stove, to enable them to observe some cooking operations, ignorant of the great danger to which they are exposing themselves and the household, in case of the ignition of the kerosene.

The crude oil, as it flows from the wells, is unfit for household purposes of illumination; it is, therefore, submitted to a process of distillation, by means of which the more inflammable portions are removed. The first product of this distillation is benzine, or benzoline, a highly inflammable and dangerous spirit. Then comes the ordinary burning oil. This, if it is properly prepared, will neither explode nor give off inflammable vapor, at ordinary temperature, and, therefore, it is perfectly safe to use in the various kinds of lamps prepared for burning it.

A very simple way of testing kerosene oil is, to pour a little into a saucer, and apply a lighted match to the surface. If the oil is suitable for lamps, it will not ignite, and, on dipping the match into the oil, the flame will be extinguished; but, if it is not highly refined, it will, at once, take fire. To try this experiment, it is better to put the saucer containing the oil, into a basin of cold water.

It is purely a fallacy to suppose that even crude mineral oils are, of themselves, explosive; they are inflammable, of course, and will burn furiously, if ignited; but the explosion is to be feared only when the petroleum vapor becomes mixed with the atmosphere, and is brought into contact with flame.

Still it should be remembered that the oil is of inflammable nature, and, if possible, it should be stored out of the house, for fear of fire. As in many other things, the rage for cheapness has led some tradesmen to purchase and sell a low grade of oil, the use of which is always attended with some risk; but refining is so constantly practiced lately, that there is little danger.

To Preserve Steel Ornaments.

The best way to preserve steel ornaments of any kind—combs, earrings, brooches, bracelets, etc.—from rust, is to pound some starch in a mortar, and sift it through fine muslin, and half fill a card-board box with it; then put in the ornaments and cover them with the starch. When they are wanted for use, brush off the starch, with a fine jewelry brush. Always put them back when not in use, and they cannot become rusted.

To Cut Pencils for Drawing.

This is not quite so trifling a matter to some, as at first it appears; for, when much delicate drawing is done, which requires a constantly clean point, and, at the same time, very clean fingers, a great deal of the incessant scraping of the knife can be avoided by cutting away the wood from several pencils before commencing, and having a sheet of fine sand-paper, on which to rub the lead to a point. It will be found a quick and sure method, and does not require one to touch the lead; but the pencil should revolve in the fingers while being rubbed.

An Excellent Method for Cleaning Silks, however Light in Color.

Boil down a pair of old, but not much soiled light kid-gloves, with a pint of water, until it is reduced to one-third of a pint, and nothing remains of the gloves, but a little pulpy substance. Then let the mixture cool, and apply with a large piece of flannel, on both sides of the silk. Shake each breadth, roll it separately in a towel, let it lie for six hours, then iron, on the wrong side, with a moderately hot iron.

To Make a Hortus Siccus.

Turn the contents of your tin-collecting case on to a newspaper, and carefully select and arrange the plants, removing all dead and fading leaves. Then, having ascertained the class and order, spread each plant on to sheets of white paper—large glazed foolscap paper is now considered the best, because blotting-paper, which has been usually supposed to be better adapted to the purpose, absorbs the colors of the leaves and flowers, while the glazed paper preserves them. Cover the plants with another sheet of paper, and spread out more plants on that, one layer above the other—press with heavy books.

Change the papers every day; have two sets of papers, and carefully dry the damp sheets before using them. Be very careful to spread every leaf and petal as flat as possible. When quite dry, affix each specimen to a sheet of paper, by pasting tiny strips of paper across the stems. The classes or orders, and the place in which it was obtained, and date, should be neatly written under each specimen.

Contamination from Zinc Tanks.

M. Zinrek calls the attention of housekeepers, in *Dingler's Polytechnic Journal*, to the fact that water, kept in small reservoirs lined with zinc, or collected from roofs covered with zinc, is, invariably, contaminated with that metal, and that the use of such water for domestic purposes, is highly injurious to health. *M. Zinrek* recommends that, where zinc tanks are employed, they should be painted over with an iron pigment.

How to Make Home Happy.

It is practicable to make home so delightful that children will have no disposition to wander from it, or prefer any other place; it is, also, possible to make it so attractive that it shall not only firmly hold its own loved ones, but shall draw others, by the power of its attractions, into its cheerful circle.

Let the house be, all day long, the scene of pleasant looks, pleasant words, kind and affectionate acts; let the table be the happy meeting-place of a merry group, and not a dull board, where a silent, if not a sullen company of animals come to be fed; let the meal be the time when a cheerful laugh is heard, and good things are said, and all the droll and pleasing incidents of the day are related.

Let the sitting-room, at evening, be the place where the smiling company enjoy themselves with newspapers, books, games and work of various kinds, until the time for the good-night kisses arrives.

Let there be music in the household, not music kept like silks and satins, rare china and silver, to exhibit to company, but home music, in which father and mother, and sister and brother, can join.

Let your companions be warmly welcomed whenever they enter the house, and be taken into the family circle, and made a part of the home group, so that daughters will not think it more agreeable to seek the obscurity of the back-parlors with their intimate friends, or to expect fathers and mothers and the younger children to leave the room, when their visitors enter it. In a word, let the house be filled with an atmosphere of cosy and cheerful good-will; then your children need not be exhorted to love it; but, on the contrary, they can hardly be tempted to leave it; and, in years to come, they will ever cherish blissful remembrances of the beloved home of their youth.

To Drive off Vermin.

Scatter Cayenne pepper all over the pantry shelves, and not an ant will molest you.

Domestic Account-Keeping.

The unsuspected extravagances, and unintentional wastefulness, which render so many poor households even poorer than they need be, are greatly owing to the custom of making purchases of supplies without any previous thought as to how the money can be expended to make it go the farthest. A little thought upon the matter, a little painstaking in the expenditures, would make a great difference in the comforts of the family.

In the same way, even in the houses of the wealthy, domestic expenses are increased from a want of arithmetical knowledge. Therefore, every girl should learn how to keep a ledger, to balance a cash-book, and to calculate averages, so as to estimate rates of expenditures, weekly, monthly and yearly. Women are usually excellent accountants, if they are bred to it from childhood; and, when a wife has a given amount for weekly or monthly expenses, she will soon learn not to waste her money upon follies; and it becomes a real pleasure to her to make the most of what she receives; and she will soon learn to manage her affairs so that there is always a margin for unexpected demands upon her allowance.

To Apply French Furniture Polish.

Make a wad with a piece of coarse flannel or drugget, by rolling it round and round; over which, on the side to be used to polish, put a bit of fine, soft linen, several times doubled up. Sew it on tightly; then moisten the wad with the preparation, by shaking the bottle and holding the wad to the mouth of it. Proceed to rub your furniture in a circular direction, doing a very little at once. Rub it lightly until the whole surface is covered; repeat this two or three times, but let each coat be rubbed until thoroughly dry, and be careful to only moisten the rag a little at a time, and you will have a very bright and lasting polish. Be also particular to keep your wad soft and clean, as the polish depends very much on the care you take to keep it clean and free from dust while rubbing and drying.

To Clean Black Cloth or Silk from Spots of Wax.

Place a little soft-soap upon each spot, and warm it, either in the sun or before the fire, slightly. Wash off, and it will disappear. Or, scrape off the wax, and cover the spot with alcohol, and rub with a soft rag.

To Clean Plate.

Take an ounce each of cream of tartar, muriate of soda, and alum, and boil in a gallon of water for ten minutes. Put in the pieces of plate or silver, and

HOUSEHOLD HINTS AND RECIPES.

Boil them for ten minutes. Take them out, and wipe slightly with a soft linen towel; then rub them dry with a chamois skin. The plate will have a beautiful silvery whiteness. Powdered magnesia will also polish silver handsomely; but, if very much tarnished, the above method is the best.

To Clean Glasses, Bottles and Decanters.

Break up a few egg-shells that have not been cooked, into the articles to be cleaned, and pour in a little cold water; if greasy, take warmish water, with a little sal-soda. Shake well; rinse out with a plenty of cold water, and let them drain thoroughly. This is the method used in the south of France. Another way is to put in spent tea-leaves, and shake them up and down with a good deal of water. They will take off all stains.

To Prevent Hair Falling Off.

Glycerine and tincture of capsicum, each two ounces; oil of bergamot, one drachm; mix well, and apply a small quantity, by rubbing it into the scalp thoroughly every night. Wash the head occasionally, with soft water and toilette soap.

How to Crimp the Hair.

To make the hair stay in crimp, take five-cents' worth of gum-arabic, and add to it just enough boiling water to dissolve it. When melted, turn in alcohol enough to make a thin fluid. Put this on the hair at night, after it is done up in crimping pins, or paper, and it will keep it in crimp the hottest day, while it cannot injure the hair.

To Prevent Doors from Creaking.

Apply a little soft-soap to the hinges; or, take lard, soap and black lead, equal parts, and apply with a brush; or, take the oil-can from the sewing-machine, and drop a few drops into the hinges.

To Clean Silk.

Dust the garment thoroughly, then rip apart, and spread an old sheet over a large table, laying the breadths of silk upon it. Take half a tea-cup of ox-gall, half a tea-cup of aqua-ammonia, made by dissolving a piece of carbonate of ammonia, as large as a walnut, in half a tea-cup of hot water. Add to this a tea-cup of tepid water.

Sponge the silk, taking care to rub out all the soiled places—wet it well on both sides. Having finished sponging, roll it on a round stick, like a broom-handle, taking care not to wrinkle it at all. Silk thus cleansed and thoroughly dried, needs no ironing, and has a lustre like new silk. Take care to shake all the moisture out, by snapping it again and again. Let two persons take hold of each breadth, and shake them, as one folds sheets to iron.

Not only silk but merino, barege, or any woolen goods can be cleaned by this method.

How Much to Eat.

In order to keep the body healthy, food should be consumed judiciously. Of course the harder a man works the more he exhausts his physical capacities, and the more nourishment he requires; and while a laboring man would need five pounds of solid mixed food daily, persons of sedentary habits, *i. e.*, those who remain quietly indoors the greater part of the time, and sleep more than eight hours out of the twenty-four, two and a half pounds would be quite sufficient. It has been ascertained that life can be sustained for two or three weeks on two ounces of food a day.

Change of food should always follow change of seasons.

In Winter we require the most stimulating food, such as is contained in fat meats, and sweets of all kinds.

In Summer fresh fruits of all kinds, fresh fish, and meats of white flesh are more desirable. Milk and eggs nourish the blood; potatoes and cereals of all kinds increase the adipose tissues. Tea and coffee are usually healthful stimulants in both Summer and Winter, if not taken to excess. It is usually better to eat too little than too much. An excessive use of animal food must surely be acknowledged as one of our national weaknesses. In many families it is the chief article of diet at breakfast, luncheon, and dinner, and often at supper also.

Now for the consolation of those who cannot afford to eat meat, in this wholesale manner, it cannot be too widely known that all the conditions of a good, nutritious diet can be found in a much cheaper form.

In oatmeal porridge and milk, for instance, they are to be met with as well as in beef or mutton.

We would not imply that one should not eat meat as a constant article of diet, if he can afford it, but that it is not of any greater use to the system than some other articles, which can be obtained at much cheaper rates.

"We are neither," says a high authority, better fed, nor stronger because our average consumption of meat is, even at its present price, greater than that of any European nation.

The chief food of the Roman gladiator, was barley-cakes and oil; and this diet, says Hippocrates, is eminently fitted to give muscular strength and endurance. The Roman soldier had little or no meat. His daily rations were one pound of barley, three ounces of oil, and a pint of thin wine.

How to Make New Rope Pliable.

Many of our readers doubtless understand how difficult it is to handle new ropes, and every farmer knows how unmanageable a new stiff rope-halter always is, and how severely his patience is tried when he endeavors to tie up the cattle with it, as the rope will coil itself into every shape but the right one; and often he will find the horses and cattle straying about the barn from having loosened the knots of the new halters. By simply boiling the rope for an hour or so all this annoyance can be avoided, and the rope becomes as soft and pliable as if used for months. Its strength is not diminished by the boiling, but its stiffness is wholly gone. It must hang in a warm room, however, until thoroughly dried, and not be allowed to kink up at all.

To Clean Knives.

Scrape at one end of the knife-board a little heap of Bath brick; rub on to a bit of wet flannel a little yellow soap; lay the knife flat on the board; dip the soaped flannel into the brick-dust, and rub it on to the knife. When clean wash the knives in a jug of warm water, but be careful not to let it touch the handle. This method saves the knives, as well as the labor of cleansing them.

How to Mend Old Pails and Buckets.

All housekeepers know that pails are forever losing their handles, and those that are used in the stables and barns, are especially addicted to this infirmity.

Just at the wrong moment the handle will break out, and although the bucket is perfectly good, it is worthless without it, and one cannot be readily furnished either by the farmer or hostler.

But whoever possesses an old boot-leg, or a strip of harness-leather, has a remedy close at hand, as they can be cut into suitable lengths, and holes punched through the upper part of the strip, which will hold the bale firmly; then tack the leather to each side of the pail, and it is as good as new. If the bale is lost, an old piece of rope can be substituted for it.

By this simple contrivance butter firkins can be made into useful pails or buckets. It will give another year's wear to many a broken pail, and prove the truth of the old adage, that *"A penny saved is a penny earned."*

How to Dry Herbs.

Herbs, when hung up to dry in loose bundles, will soon lose their odor. They should be thinly spread out on newspapers, in a warm place, but shaded from the sun; and when well dried, pressed together, and put into paper bags. It is a good plan to strip off the leaves, and rub them fine through a sieve, and put into wide-mouthed bottles, and label them. Gather them just before they commence to flower.

To Make Mats from Sheepskins.

A fresh sheepskin can be more easily prepared than one that is a little dry. Make a strong soap-suds, then let the water cool so as to be lukewarm. In the mean time pick out all the dirt from the wool that can be pulled off. Then dip it into the soap-suds, and scrub the wool on the wash-board. A table-spoonful of kerosene added to three gallons of the suds will greatly assist you in making the wool soft and white. Wash in another suds, and change the water again, if the wool is not clean.

Then put the skin into cold water enough to cover it, and dissolve half a pound of salt, and the same quantity of alum, in three pints of boiling water; pour the mixture over the skin side, and rinse it up and down in the water. Let it soak in the same water for twelve hours, then hang it over a fence or strong line to drain. When the water ceases to drip, stretch it upon a board to dry, or nail it on the wall of the wood-house or barn, wool side toward the board; when nearly dry, rub into the skin, one ounce each of powdered alum and saltpetre mixed together; if the skin is large, use double the quantity. Rub this in for an hour; you can do it easier by putting the skin on to a table. Then fold the skin sides together, and hang it away; do this for three days. Then scrape off all impurities with a blunt knife, and rub the skin with salt and alum, and in a week or two it is ready for use.

How to Hang Pictures.

Pictures should not be hung higher than the height of the average human eye, when the owner of the eye is standing. It is the almost universal rule, in our houses, to hang pictures much above this level; and to enjoy them one is obliged to look upwards, in a very wearisome manner.

If the picture is a portrait, or if it have human faces in it, the eyes should look as nearly into ours as possible; and if there be no such simple guide, perhaps a good rule will be to have the line that divides the picture horizontally into equal parts, level with the eye.

If one starts in hanging pictures with the determination to place them so that they can be seen easily, and enjoyed without stretching the neck in the least, he will be quite sure to succeed in putting them in a good position. In country taverns and farm-houses we often see pictures skyed as high as if their owners had been Academy hangers, and the painters young rivals of a new school. Very likely the reason is that the picture is a precious possession, and should therefore be hung, securely, out of the reach of children's hands, or those of meddlers who desire to touch everything they behold.

But as people learn to enjoy pictures, and to receive spiritual and intellectual nourishment from them, they will desire to have them where they can be the most readily seen.

Newspapers for Warm Covering for Cold Nights, Etc.

On cold nights, when the bed clothing does not seem sufficient, you can adopt this simple plan, and find decided comfort in it.

Throw off the counterpane, and spread two or three large newspapers over the bed, then replace the cover.

The result will be a warm and comfortable night, without any perceptible weight of the bedding.

If you are to take a cold ride in carriage or boat, or a long walk against the wind, spread a newspaper over your chest before you button up your overcoat, and you will not be chilled to your bones.

Nothing can be cheaper, and nothing more efficacious.

If your feet are cold during the day, wrap newspapers tightly outside of your stockings, and then put on your boots, and you will be surprised at their warmth.

When the mercury falls far down in the thermometer, tuck newspapers behind the plants in the windows, and the frost will not harm them.

To Transfer Engravings on Wood.

Varnish the wood evenly with common white varnish, such as is often called map varnish. Cut off the margin of the engravings or pictures, which should be on unsized paper, that is, paper that absorbs water like blotting paper. Wet the back of the print with a damp sponge, using only enough water to saturate the paper, but not so wet as to moisten the printed surface.

Then, with a flat camel's hair brush, give it a coat of transfer varnish, which is made by dissolving copal varnish in spirits of wine, on the printed side, and apply it immediately, varnished side downwards, on to the wood work. Place a sheet of paper over it and press it down with the hand until every part adheres.

Then gently rub away the back of the print with the fingers, till nothing but the engraving or colors remain. It may need to be wetted again, before all the paper can be removed, but if it is too wet it will be spoiled. Great care is needed in this operation that the design be not disturbed. When the pulp of the paper is taken off, let it dry, and give it a coat of the spirits of wine varnish, and it will appear as if printed on the wood.

How to Prevent Cold Feet.

Draw off your stockings, when retiring at night, and rub your ankles and feet with a flesh brush or with your hand, as hard as you can bear the pressure, for ten minutes, and you will never complain of cold feet in bed.

It is hardly conceivable what a pleasurable glow such a rubbing will produce.

Frequent bathing of the feet in the morning, and rubbing them thoroughly dry with a coarse linen or flannel cloth, is also very useful for this trouble.

An extra sole in the boot or shoe is also desirable. If one is troubled with cold feet during the day, it is an excellent plan to scatter red pepper,

(Cayenne,) into the stockings, not letting it blister the feet, but only warm the skin.

Cold feet, habitually, is one of the sure avenues to death, and care should be taken to keep up a good circulation of the blood, both by rubbing and tonics.

How to Ventilate Rooms and Large Halls.

Ventilation is not so difficult a matter as it is generally imagined; but for want of a little knowledge on the subject, many serious blunders are often committed. Where gas or kerosene is consumed for lighting a room, a large amount of carbonic acid and water is generated, and this takes place in every lighted room, even if candles are used alone. And the result is this: The hydrogen of the gas, or oil, unites with the oxygen of the air, taking eight measures of oxygen to one of itself to form nine measures of water, which is deposited on the windows and walls, if provision is not made for its escape; then the carbon unites with a portion of the oxygen to form carbonic acid gas, by weight of the carbon combining with sixteen parts by weight of oxygen.

In the ventilation of large rooms, churches, concert halls, etc., it is desirable to have shafts to admit fresh air, and escapes for the foul air. A plan has been introduced of late years, which consists in admitting a current of fresh air at the upper part on one side, according to the direction of the wind; that on the right of the room entering by the skirting-board, which is pierced with small holes, or narrow slits, one-sixteenth of an inch in width, and nearly the depth of the skirting; and that on the left passing through the floor.

The outlet for the vitiated air is placed in the center of the ceiling over the chandeliers, and this is provided with a valve which opens upwards; above this is a gas light which rarifies the air, and so draws up the foul air from the room in the same manner that a cupping glass draws the blood from the body.

The chief points requiring attention in ventilating rooms or halls, consists in having an inlet for fresh air and an outlet for vitiated air. The air should be admitted as fresh and pure as possible, and free from local vitiations, such as drains, smoke of manufactories, and the like. When air is admitted into a room, it should be at the lowest part, and the aggregate area of admission, should be twice as great as that of the outlet. When there are galleries in a hall, church, or the like, they should be supplied with fresh air from the outside of the building, and not from the body of the room. Air can be warmed when admitted into a large hall, by making it pass over pipes filled with hot water. All ventilating shafts, or chimneys, should be as smooth inside as possible, as every projection impedes the currents of air.

Ventilation is needed even in stables and cow-houses, and the want of this essential preservation of health, occasions much suffering, both mentally and bodily.

The Fine Art of Patching and Darning.

To patch!—how vulgar a term it is thought to be in these days of elegant wardrobes, when some ladies esteem it the height of their ambition to outshine their neighbors in exquisite toilettes. Yet patching is an operation that requires far more skill than does the making of a new garment, and, when it is well done, it may save the purchase of many a costly one; for the most expensive dress may, by some untoward accident, be torn or defaced badly, the first day it is worn, and if a piece can be inserted, or if it can be so darned that it is hardly discernible, it will be a great saving of expense.

If the material is striped or figured, the pattern should be exactly matched; then a tiny slit must be made in each corner, to make the seam lay down flat, and there must not be the least approach to a pucker; and the kind of seam should be such as will be least apparent; a very fine running stitch is the best, if no wear comes upon it. Is not this an art which requires both teaching and experience, to become a proficient in it?

So of darning, much instruction is needful as to the number of threads to be left by the needle, according to the kind of fabric; then there is the kind of thread or yarn most suitable, which requires some experience to determine. When the article is coarse, the chief attention should be directed to expedition, but a costly article of embroidery on muslin, or lace, can only be well darned with ravelings of the same muslin. Such particulars do not come to a girl by inspiration, but they must be taught, or left to be acquired by dearly bought experience.

The third mode of repair is well understood and practiced by the French and German women, though rarely in this country.

To be able to darn finely, is really an accomplishment, and the various stitches that are taught by fine needle-women, are not any more difficult or tedious to execute, than any kind of embroidery.

The stocking-stitch, for instance, can repair the finest of thread or silk stockings perfectly. And if a lady pays four or five dollars for a handsome pair of stockings, it is quite essential that she should know how to repair them.

Practice in lace stitches is also desirable, for the deficiency of a single loop, when lace is washed, often makes a large hole during the operation, and the value of the lace is destroyed.

And the shawl-stitch, by using it with ravelings from the shawl itself, the most costly cashmere can be repaired without a possibility of discovering the rent. To be an expert in such useful works should surely merit as much commendation, as to excel in crochet or fancy work of any kind.

In our large cities, it might well answer to establish schools where the art of mending, in all its finest as well as plainest branches, should be the chief object of instruction; and three months, or less, of lessons, if taken two or three times a week, would make any girl an adept in the occupation, if she were a good plain needle-woman at the commencement.

The sewing-machines have not been a blessing to the rising generation, for young girls have not been taught to hem, fell, and sew over and over, as were their grandmothers and mothers. Yet without a practical knowledge of these things, no lady can judge whether her seamstress has done a reasonable quantity of sewing in a given time, even if she can tell whether it is well done. And if this be true as to plain sewing, it is still more applicable to mending of all kinds.

To Extract Grease Spots from Silks, Muslins, Etc.

Take a piece of French chalk, hold it over the spot, and scrape a little of it directly upon the grease. Then hold it near the fire, or over a bowl of boiling water, and the grease will become softened, and absorbed by the chalk, brush or rub it off, repeat if it is not all extracted.

Chloroform will also remove all grease spots.

To Clean Marble.

Take two parts of saleratus or common soda; one part of powdered pumice-stone; and one part of very finely powdered chalk; sift them all together through a sieve, and mix into a stiff paste with water. Rub it hard all over the marble, until the stains are removed.

Then wash off with soap and water, and the marble will be beautifully clean.

To Perfume Linen.

Take one pound of rose leaves dried in the shade; one ounce each of cloves, allspice, and caraway seeds. Grind the spices fine in a mortar, add a quarter of a pound of best table salt, mix well together, and put into little bags, and lay them in the linen drawers.

To Remove Ink or Fruit Stains from the Fingers.

Take half an ounce of salts of sorrel, and the same quantity of cream of tartar, both powdered fine, mix and keep in a bottle tightly corked. This is what is called salts of lemon, and when the fingers are damp, shake a little of the powder upon them, and rub off with a nail brush.

To Prevent Iron and Steel from Rusting.

Take two parts of the chloride of iron, the crystallized; and two parts of chloride of antimony, and one part of gallic acid; and dissolve the whole into four parts of water. Give the iron or steel two separate coatings by rubbing it on with a woolen cloth, and dry it each time in the sun, but not by any artificial heat.

When it is thoroughly dried, wash it over with warm water, and let it dry again. Then in twenty-four hours apply linseed oil, well boiled, mixed with one part to ten of turpentine.

Let this dry well before handling, and it will be found to withstand the action of moisture and dampness; and it is of a handsome chocolate brown color.

The more coats that are applied of the first mixture, the deeper will be the color produced.

For machinery, fences, and all exposed portions of steel and iron, this compound will be found to be invaluable.

To Keep Leather Harnesses Pliable.

It is well-known that leather articles which are kept in stables are liable to become hardened by the ammoniacal exhalations, which not only affect the harnesses but also the shoes of those who frequent the stables. The usual applications of grease will not always prove equal to meet this difficulty, but if a small quantity of glycerine is added to the grease spot, the leather will be kept continually in a soft and pliable condition.

To Wash Ribbons, Silk Handkerchiefs, Etc.

A good quality of satin ribbon can be made to look very well if washed first in cold water, to which is added half a tea-spoonful of alcohol; then a weak lather made of lukewarm water and white soap; afterward rinse in cold water, pull even, and dry gradually. To iron the ribbon, lay it within a sheet of clear, smooth letter paper, and press it with a moderately heated iron, moved over it quickly. If the color is lilac, add a little dissolved pearlash to the rinsing water. If green, a little vinegar. If pink or blue, a few drops of oil of vitriol. If yellow, a little of the tincture of saffron.

Other colors can be set by stirring a tea-spoonful of ox-gall into the first water. If white, a salt-spoonful of cream of tartar should be mixed with the soap-suds.

Silk handkerchiefs and scarfs can be washed and ironed in the same manner. If the colors are delicate, use only the alcohol and the ox-gall.

The proportion of alcohol is about a table-spoonful to a gallon of water.

Cement for the Mouths of Corked Bottles.

Melt together a quarter of a pound of sealing-wax, the same quantity of resin, and two ounces of bees-wax.

When it froths stir it with a tallow candle. As soon as it becomes liquid, dip into it the mouths of the corked bottles.

This is the very best way to exclude the air from such liquids as are injured by being exposed to it.

A good cement for bottles and jars can be made by melting half a pound of tallow, with quarter of a pound of resin, and proceed as above.

How to Pack Household Articles.

In packing for removal to a distant place, let all the boxes and trunks be numbered, and the numbers written down on a sheet of paper.

Some one person should superintend the whole of the packing, and keep an exact account of every article, and also of the box or trunk in which it is packed, and the order in which they are placed.

It will be found to be of great assistance in unpacking, for by consulting the list you will readily find whatever you desire, and will know exactly which one of the packing cases should be opened first.

If you are going to take a long sea voyage, this method of packing will be found very convenient, for if you need any particular article, a glance at your list will inform you in which trunk it will be found.

If the list is kept in a little blank book, it will be more easily procured when needed.

To Wash Vials.

Put a quart or more of fresh ashes into an iron kettle, and pour over it a gallon of cold water. Put it over the fire, lay in the vials, mouths downward, and let it gradually heat to a boiling point. After it has boiled ten or fifteen minutes take off the kettle, and set it aside until nearly or quite cold.

Then take out the vials, and rinse in cold water, and drain, wiping dry the outsides.

Black glass bottles can be cleansed in the same manner. If you desire to cleanse a single vial, put into it a little pinch of saleratus, and then turn in with a funnel, some warm water and shake it violently; let it stand awhile, then turn out, and rinse in warm water. If it still has a bad odor repeat the operation.

To Clean Silk of all Kinds.

Pare and slice or grate fine three potatoes that have been well washed. Pour over them half a pint of boiling water, and let it stand until cold. Strain off the water, and add an equal quantity of spirits of wine.

Sponge the silk on the right side with the mixture, rubbing it hard, and when half dry, iron it on the wrong side, putting a piece of thin tissue paper over the silk to keep the iron from making it shine.

By this process the most delicately colored silks can be cleaned, and made to look like new.

To Iron Velvet.

Place a towel of several thicknesses, thoroughly wetted, over the heated side of a smoothing iron. Lay over it the wrong side of the velvet, and pass a small whisk brush, such as is used to brush and dust velvet and crape, over the pile, until the surface is smooth and looks fresh.

To Renew Scorched or Browned Linen.

It is not an easy thing to take out stains made by scorching hot flat-irons, and often garments are entirely ruined by them, but the following process is more successful than any other yet known. Take a quart of vinegar, and boil it with half a dozen large onions, for half an hour. Strain off the liquor, and add to it a large table-spoonful of bar soap scraped up fine, a quarter of a pound of Fullers' earth, one table-spoonful of slacked lime, and one of saleratus. Mix all these ingredients together, and turn the vinegar over them slowly, then boil the mixture until it is quite thick; and lay it over the scorched part. Then put the article in the sun, and as the paste dries, wet it with a little water. Thus treated the stain often disappears in a few hours, but if not, repeat the process.

To Clean Japanned Waiters, Urns, Etc.

Rub on, with a sponge, a little white soap, and some lukewarm water, and wash the waiter or urn until quite clean. Never use hot water, as it will cause the Japan varnish to scale off. Having wiped it dry, sprinkle a little flour over it; let it stand awhile, and then wipe it off with a soft bit of flannel, and polish it with the flannel, or with a silk handkerchief.

If there are white heat marks on the waiters, you will hardly be able to remove them entirely, but you can rub them with sweet oil and a piece of flannel, and then put on a little spirits of wine.

Papier mache waiters, and all articles of similar manufacture, should be first washed with a sponge and cold water, without soap, and then sprinkle flour over them, while damp, and in ten or fifteen minutes rub it off, and polish by hard rubbing.

To Remove Black Stains from the Skin.

Take half an ounce of oxalic acid, and half an ounce of cream of tartar; mix and pulverize to the finest powder, and put into a glass bottle labeled "Poison."

When the skin has been discolored from wearing black crape, or other articles of mourning, dip the corner of a towel into a little water, sprinkle on a little of the mixture, and rub it on the place, then wash it off *at once*, and afterwards wash with soap and water, and the black stains will have disappeared.

This mixture will also remove ink stains, and all other spots from the fingers, and from white clothing and table linen. It will act more speedily if the towel is wetted with boiling water.

As oxalic acid is a deadly **poison**, care **must** be taken to keep the bottle out of the way of children.

The Uses of Ammonia in the Household.

No housekeeper should be without a bottle of spirits of ammonia, for besides its medical value, it is also invaluable for many household purposes. It is nearly as useful an article, for all cleansing uses, as soap, and its cheapness, brings it within the means of all.

Turn a tea-spoonful of ammonia into a quart of warm soap-suds; dip in a bit of flannel, and wipe off the grim, and smoke, and dust, from any painted woodwork, and see for yourselves, how much hard labor it will save you, for you do not need to scrub it with all your strength, only wipe it off.

It will also clean and brighten silver wonderfully. Mix a tea-spoonful of the ammonia with a pint of hot suds; dip in your silver forks and spoons, rub them with a soft brush, and polish with a chamois skin, and you will use it weekly, if not oftener.

For washing mirrors and windows it is very excellent. Put a few drops of the ammonia upon a bit of newspaper, and you can rub off any marks upon the glass at once.

It will also take out grease spots from all kinds of cloth. Mix a few drops with a few drops of water, and rub gently on the spot; lay a blotting paper over the place, and press a moderately heated flat-iron upon it, and it will disappear. A few drops turned upon a wetted towel, and gently pressed upon the edge of a soiled collar, will whiten it.

Then it is a most refreshing agent for the toilette, for a few drops in a basin of water, will remove all disagreeable odors of the skin. If a tea-spoonful is added to a foot-bath, it will take away all unpleasantness from the feet. And there is nothing better for cleansing the hair from dust and dandruff, than half a tea-spoonful of ammonia in a tea-cupful of warm water.

For cleaning hair and nail brushes, it is equally good. Put a tea-spoonful of it into a pint of warm water, and dip the brushes into the water and scrub them well; then shake out until nearly dry, and put into the sunshine. The most soiled brushes will come forth from such a bath white and clean.

For medicinal purposes ammonia is much used. In cases of severe headache, it will prove a very agreeable remedy, and a frequent inhalation of its pungent vapors, will often cure a catarrhal cold. There is no better remedy than aromatic spirits of ammonia for a severe cough. Twenty drops of it, taken in a wine-glass of water, will frequently prove of great relief. It is also a good remedy for dyspepsia and heart-burn. The common spirits of ammonia can be used in the same way, but it is not as palatable as the aromatic spirits.

In addition to all these uses, ammonia can be applied to vegetation with most beneficial effects. If you desire to make your roses, fuchsias, geraniums, and carnations blossom, add half a tea-spoonful of the ammonia to every pint and a half of warm water, and sprinkle them with it. But do not use it oftener than twice a week.

HOUSEHOLD HINTS AND RECIPES.

Rain water is impregnated with ammonia, and it is more refreshing and invigorating than spring water, to vegetable life.

Ammonia should always be kept tightly closed with a glass stopper, as it is so strong, that it eats away a cork.

To Make Pomade.

Those of our lady readers who cultivate flowers, can, from the following directions, prepare a very fragrant pomade.

Place any suitable utensil in a bowl of hot water, and fill it with pure clarified fat, either well boiled lard free from salt, or beef's marrow boiled for several hours in water, and then strained through a cloth.

Keep the bowl on the back part of the stove or range, so as to have the fat in a liquid state all the time, but not boiling hot. Then put in as many flowers and leaves as you can fill into the bowl, and let them remain in it for twenty-four hours, and strain off the fat, and add more flowers. Continue this process for six or eight days, and the fat will be highly scented.

If you desire the perfume of roses, take their leaves, or those of the tube-rose, mignonnette, heliotrope, etc., etc., using only one kind of flower for one dish of fat.

If you desire it in a liquid state, cut the fat with alcohol.

The object of putting the vessel containing the fat into the bowl of water, is to prevent the fat from burning. If the bowl is filled with fine sand, kept well heated, it will do as well, if not better.

Javelle Water for Taking Out Stains.

Javelle water, such as is prepared by druggists, can be easily made at home, and it will take out stains from both linen and cotton.

Take one pound of sal-soda, and five or six cents worth of chloride of lime; put them in an earthen bowl, and turn over them two quarts of boiling hot water—the softer the better—rain water is the best. Let it settle, then pour off; bottle and keep for use. It will remove fruit stains, and even take out indelible ink spots. When used, soak the stain till it disappears. Then wash it in water.

How to Extinguish Clothes on Fire.

Three persons out of four will rush up to the burning individual, and commence to tear off their clothing without any definite aim, and call for water, without effecting any good.

The only way is to take any woolen material, the blanket from a bed, the rug at your feet, *anything*, and hold the corners as wide apart as possible, and run up to the sufferer and wrap it tightly about him, folding your arms close about the shoulders or limbs where the fire predominates. This will instantly smother the fire and save the face. Then throw the person on the floor, and the rest of the flame can then be extinguished.

Then immerse the burned surfaces in cold water, and keep them closely covered with wetted bandages.

Common wheat flour should then be sprinkled over the burns, to the thickness of an inch, and if possible, keep the patient in bed, and give an anodyne of some kind. If badly burned, by all means send for a physician, for the shock to the nervous system may be greater than you can imagine.

If the physician is not needed, let the flour be undisturbed until it falls off of itself, when a new skin will have formed under it. Unless the burns are very deep, no other remedies will be needed.

Dry flour, for burns, is the most excellent remedy ever proposed, and every housewife should so understand it. The principle of its action is, like water, it causes relief from pain, by excluding all the air from the inflamed surfaces.

An Excellent Recipe for Whitewash.

The following recipe for whitewash is recommended by the *Scientific American*, and it will answer for wood, brick, stone, or mortar.

Slack about one-half a bushel of fresh lime, with boiling water, keeping the pail or bucket that contains it covered during the process. Strain it, and add a peck of salt dissolved in warm water, three pounds of ground rice that has been boiled to a thin paste, one-half a pound of powdered Spanish whiting, and one pound of clear glue, dissolved in warm water. Mix all these ingredients thoroughly together, and let the mixture stand for several days. Then heat it in a kettle over a portable furnace, if possible, and put it on as hot as it can be handled, either with whitewashers' or painters' brushes.

It can be colored yellow with chrome-yellow, and brown with Spanish brown and a little lamp black.

A Good Recipe for a Cheap Paint.

Take eleven pounds of fresh, dry lime, sifted fine, one gallon of water, two gallons of linseed oil, raw or boiled, one-fourth pound of potash dissolved in a pint of water, boiling hot.

First mix your lime and water, until it is like a thick hasty pudding. Then add the oil and potash water.

Stir up thoroughly, and if the oil and water unite, it is ready for use; if not, a little more potash water should be added to cut the oil. Use no more potash than is needful for this purpose. Put on with a paint brush, like other paint.

It will appear much thicker than common oil paint, but it will lay on better in this condition. It has been well tried, and with the best effects. It wears well, and will cost less than half the price of white lead paint.

HOUSEHOLD HINTS AND RECIPES.

Don't Borrow.

A housekeeper can cultivate few habits that are worse than that of borrowing. It is a practice that often serves to destroy pleasant neighborhoods, and in the end breaks up friendships. While, if a little fore-thought is practiced, there will be no need of sending to a neighbor for anything. Always look over the pantry and store-room in the morning, directly after breakfast, and see what things are needed for the day. Open the tea canister and see that there is a good supply, look into the coffee can, and into the sugar bucket, the saleratus jar, the salt box, and so on, until you know just what stores are running low, and make a memorandum of them, and see that they are obtained before the supply is wholly exhausted.

No one likes to be constantly asked for a drawing of tea, a little butter, a few slices of bread, a cup of sugar, etc., etc., etc., and yet no lady likes to refuse to do such acts of neighborly kindness. Therefore, never put your neighbor's good nature to any such test.

Very often the cook is the borrower, and the mistress knows nothing about the demands that are made upon her neighbors. Therefore, it is a good plan to tell your servant that you neither borrow nor lend, and she must on no account go to a neighbor's without your knowledge, nor lend to any one without your permission. Then you alone are responsible for the acts.

We have known of a lady (?) who borrowed a velvet dress to pattern after, and wore it to a party before she returned it.

How to make Otto of Roses.

Fill a two-gallon, glass jar with clean, freshly-picked rose leaves. Then take a two-ounce vial, and fit it inside as a cork for the jar. Cut some sponge into narrow strips; soak them in pure olive oil, free from all odor; put them into the vial, and turn it into the neck of the jar. Place them in the sun for a week or so, and the heat will distill the rose leaves, and the aroma will ascend and saturate the oil in the sponge. Put in fresh leaves four or five times, and you will have a small bottle of the finest otto of roses that can be made. Be sure to keep it tightly corked, or it will evaporate.

How to Drive.

Most drivers over-drive. They attempt too much, and in so doing distract or hamper the horse. Now and then you find a horse, with such a vicious gait, that his speed is gotten from him only by the most artificial process; but such horses are, fortunately, rare, and hence the style of management required cannot become general.

The true way is to let the horse drive himself, the driver doing little but directing him, and giving him that confidence which a horse alone gets in himself, when he feels that a guide and friend is back of him.

But the most vicious and inexcusable style of driving, is that which so many drivers adopt, viz., wrapping the lines around either hand, and pulling the horse backward with all their might and main, so that the horse, in point of fact, pulls the weight back of him with his mouth, and not with his breast and shoulders. This they do under the impression that such a dead pull is needed in order to "steady" the horse.

The fact is, with rare exceptions, there should never be any pull upon the horse at all. A steady pressure is allowable, probably advisable, but anything beyond this, has no justification in nature or reason; for nature suggests the utmost possible freedom of action of head, body and limbs, in order that the animal may attain the highest rate of speed; and reason certainly forbids the supposition that by the bits, and not by the breast-collar, the horse is to draw the weight attached to it.

In speeding my horses, I very seldom grasp the lines with both hands, when the road is straight and clear from obstructions. The lines are rarely steadily taut, but held in easy pliancy, and used chiefly to shift the bit in the animal's mouth, and by this motion communicate courage and confidence to him.

Rev. W. H. H. MURRAY.

Various Styles of Draperies for Windows.

Tasteful and inexpensive styles of window curtains have lately been introduced, that will gratify the æsthetic tastes of those housekeepers, whose incomes will not allow them to indulge in rich tapestry or velvet hangings. It is pleasing, also, to see a cheaper mode of decoration, even in the homes of the wealthy, and materials which were formerly never supposed suitable for window draperies, are now employed with fine effect.

These curtains can also be made at home, and each lady can exercise her own taste upon their manufacture, and strive to produce original designs in ornamenting them.

Window draperies have always been considered desirable, not alone for their usefulness, but also for the elegance they give to the appearance of any room; and their effectiveness as background or shadow have always been considered essential to its completeness. The harmony of color, however, should be as carefully studied in the matter of curtains, as in the toilette of a modern belle.

We do not know what ingenious mind first suggested the use of Turkish toweling for window draperies, but it has been the fashion for several years, by the aid of artistically selected shades of velvet, brocade, or even flannel, applied in bands, or by *cretonne* embroidery, to cut out bright flowers, figures, or birds, from handsome French *cretonnes,* and apply them to the toweling by a button-hole stitch, worked in colored silks or worsteds.

The curtains are banded across the tops and bottoms, and the bands are put on with feather-stitch in silks or worsteds of the same color as the bands, or in contrasting lines. If the *cretonne* is used, the pieces are applied either all over the curtains, or in set figures, wreaths, or vines, down the center.

The toweling can be obtained either in single or double widths, and it is so thick, that it makes most desirable draperies for winter; while lace or embroidered muslin can be substituted in the summer.

Turkish toweling has been much used, also, for furniture covering, and is worked, not only with *applique* figures, that come ready stamped for the purpose, but also with colored worsted braids, applied with a button-hole stitch in gold colored silk.

For carriage blankets it is also much in vogue, and it can be lined, if desired, with a bright colored flannel, or farmer's satin.

Gray table damask, in two colors, that is woven in diamonds or checks, with stars, flowers, or butterflies, woven in each division, has been extensively used, of late, for tidies and small table-cloths; the figures being worked in long stitch, with bright colored worsteds, mixed with black, to set off the lighter shades, and crossed over with gold colored floss, and the dividing lines chain-stitched with black, and at the corners crossed with the floss.

But now a still more desirable use for the damask has been invented, for the three yards width goods can be made up into really beautiful window curtains. Divide the damask by cutting it through the seam, allowing enough for each curtain to hang, either straight to the floor, and rest upon it a little, or else to be looped up a little.

Put a hem border of a stripe of red and white table damask, which can be used as trimming very effectively; or put a hem border of colored canton flannel, or of Turkey red, or of French blue percale.

Then embroider the lower and upper part of the curtains in a wide band, in the same manner that the tidies are worked, and edge the bands with narrow strips of cashmere, red, blue, maroon, or green, or, if you wish, with stripes of velvet or velveteen. Cut them so as to be three inches in width when stitched on with a sewing machine.

When finished the effect is really charming, and a set of curtains worked in this manner, will give an attractive air to the plainest of apartments. These curtains can be procured at the upholsterers, but they are expensive, while any lady of leisure can easily make them at home.

Burlaps, or the newly invented styles of manila cloths, make very pretty curtains, and they can also be worked in worsteds in various pleasing designs.

Borders can be worked in the same manner as the bed-room mats, that are so fashionable at present, and the edges can be fringed out, and worked in with colored worsteds.

Beautiful curtains can also be made of unbleached muslin, or cotton, as we style the cloth at the north. It may seem absurd to employ such common material for this purpose, but it needs only to be seen to be highly appreciated, and any prejudice against it will be quickly effaced.

At the large upholstering establishments in the cities, these curtains can be found trimmed with colored velvets, cashmeres, flannels, or percales and Turkey red cotton. Indeed, anything that is bright and pretty in hue, can be used for trimming them.

A nice piece of unbleached cotton, from one yard to one and a quarter, or half, in width, should be purchased, and a cheaper kind can be used for linings if desired. The ten-quarters width can also be used, and torn down the middle for the separate breadths. Allow as many yards as are needed to drape the windows gracefully.

Then, if you take flannel, which is much used on them, you can purchase scarlet, and navy blue, or dark brown, and yellow shades, and cut them into strips of an eighth of a yard in width, and baste them across the curtain about three-eighths of a yard above the hem at the bottom. The strips run across the curtains at the top and at the bottom, leaving about an inch or two between each strip. Cut the strips lengthwise of the material, to avoid seams. Put the upper strips a quarter of a yard below the cornice or top of the curtains. Finish the edges with rows of feather stitch in black, deep green, or a pale salmon color, or else stitch them on with the sewing-machine, which, although it is not nearly as pretty, can be done much more expeditiously.

The most elaborate way of making up these curtains, is to plait the material, after it has been ornamented, lined, and bound on the edge with the brightest color, upon each side of the cornice, and in the center hang a piece two yards long and one yard wide, trimmed with narrower bands of the colors, plaiting it in deep box plaits. This must be fastened to the cornice first, or if black walnut poles are used, it must be hung upon them by means of large rings of the same material, and then the side curtains can be hung under the drapery, and need not be looped back, unless it be more desirable to do so.

Colored canton flannels, in handsome shades of brown, blue, and crimson, can also be used with good effect, upon unbleached cotton, and the shaggy side be put on for the right side. They can be feather-stitched on, either with black, or yellow, worsteds or flosses. Broader bands and less in number, can be used if preferred.

Fringes can also be sewn upon the upper bands, and they are much used by the upholsterers for this purpose.

The pretty glazed chintz and *cretonnes* which come in handsome stripes of flowers, or patterns of various devices, can also be put on in bands, across the top and bottom, with a fluted edge up and down the sides; the latter can be plaited with a machine plaiter, and then stitched on to the cotton.

Canton flannel, unbleached, will also hang very prettily, and it can be ornamented with flowers, birds, or figures, such as are printed on *cretonne*, and if one desires to do the work expeditiously, they can, after being artistically grouped, be covered over with paste, on the wrong side, and then pressed on to the Canton flannel, with a moderately hot iron.

When this kind of window decoration is commenced, various designs will present themselves to the tastefully disposed, and you will be surprised at the fine effects you can produce from materials hitherto considered impracticable for such uses.

A *soupcon* of yellow, mingled with crimson, blue, or green, either as a button-holed stitch, or feather stitch, will have a charming effect; while crimson is a warm hue that is always good. Very fine color and effect can thus be given to apartments, and especially to bed-rooms, by these simple means; but if you take the paler shades of pink, blue, and Nile green, you must have perfection in furniture and pictures, to harmonize with such delicate tints.

Cornices are not so much the fashion now, as poles of black walnut, or pine stained to imitate the natural wood, with rings to match, running over them, upon which the curtains are fastened. Any carpenter can cut the poles and turn the rings for you, and you can stain or oil them yourselves. Or you can paint the poles bright vermilion, or a dark blue, and the rings in the same way.

To Destroy Ant Hills.

The following method of destroying ant hills, is given in the *Revue Horticole*, as having proved quite successful:

Take two ounces of soft soap, one pound of common potash, and one quart and half a pint of warm water. Boil the whole together for half an hour, stirring it up occasionally. Then let the mixture cool a little, and with a pointed stick make holes here and there where the soil is infested by the ants, but at a safe distance from any plants that may be growing there, to avoid the chance of injuring them with the hot fluid. Fill up the holes with it, and you will not be troubled with the ants. By this means a French gardener was completely successful in ridding his melon beds of these troublesome insects.

To Close Cracks in Stoves.

When a good stove becomes cracked, it is very convenient to know how to mend it, and we are assured that the following recipe is a reliable one:

Sift wood ashes through a fine sieve, and add to them equal quantity of finely pulverized clay, and a little fine salt. Moisten this mixture with enough water to make a stiff paste, and put it into the cracks with a small pointed stick. This cement will not peel off or break away, and will grow very hard and firm when the stove is hot. The stove must be cool when the application is made. The cement can also be used in setting the plates of a stove, or in fitting stove-pipes, as it keeps all the joints perfectly tight and secure.

To Remove Stains from Books.

The most simple, but at the same time very effectual method of erasing spots of grease, wax, oil, or any other fat substance, is by washing the part with ether and placing it between blotting paper; then with a hot iron press above the stained parts, and the defects will be speedily removed.

When the paper is disfigured with stains of iron, it may be perfectly restored by applying a solution of sulphate of potash, and afterwards one of oxalic acid. The sulphate extracts from the iron part of its oxygen, and renders it soluble in the diluted acid. In many cases where stains are fresh, a little spirits of wine will remove the blemish.

To remove spots of ink, and even writing itself, salts of lemon diluted in a little water may be applied with success, and after a few minutes wash it off with pure water.

To Clean Looking Glasses.

Take a clean sponge and dip it slightly into water, and squeeze it as dry as possible; then dip it into spirits of wine, rub it over the glass, dust it with some powdered blue or whiting sifted through muslin. Rub it off lightly and quickly with a clean cloth, and polish it with a silk handkerchief. If the glass is a large one, clean half of it at a time, or the alcohol will dry on before it can be rubbed off.

If the frames are gilded, you must be very careful not to touch them, as it will injure the gilding. To clean such frames, rub them well with a little dry cotton wool; this will take off the dust and smoke without injury to them. If gilt frames are varnished, they can be wiped over with weak tea.

To Make Boots Water-proof.

Various preparations have been made to render leather water-proof, and the following is an excellent mixture:

Melt in an earthern dish half a pint of linseed oil, one ounce of beeswax, one ounce of oil of turpentine, and half an ounce resin. Saturate the boots with this composition, and they will be not only impervious to the wet, but also pliable and soft. Boots that have been water-proofed in this way will be found very useful for occasional shooting and fishing excursions, but for every day wear they are considered unwholesome, on account of confining the feet too closely. Yet this objection can be removed by wearing cork soles, which will absorb the moisture of the feet.

Castor Oil for Harnesses, Boots, Etc.

Castor oil is the best lubricating oil that can be used to keep harnesses, boots, and the like, in an oleaginous condition. It can be applied clear and without heat, and it will make the leather soft, smooth, and less liable to absorb moisture. A little lamp-black can be mixed with it to use on old harnesses and boots, but it is seldom needed for new leather, as the oil will keep the leather black.

If you have been troubled with stiff, cracked, water-soaked boots, and the leather so shrunken and rough as to chafe the feet, if you will try castor oil you will be surprised at its efficacy. Only a very little of it is needed; put only a drop or two on to a bit of flannel, and it will moisten a good surface. For oiling wagons and buggies it is excellent, as it keeps them in good running order for a longer time than any other oil.

East Indian Method of Cleaning Silver.

The East Indian dealers in silver ware, never apply any abrasive substance to it, but for cleaning all kinds of plate, even the most delicate, the following method is employed:

Cut some large juicy lemons into thick slices, and rub the articles very briskly with them; then cover them, in a pan, with the slices of lemon, and let them stand two or three hours. Rinse them in some clear water, and put into a pan of very hot soap-suds, and stir them about in it. Take out, rinse in clear hot water, dry off, and finish by rubbing with a chamois skin.

Green tamarind pods are also excellent to clean gold and silver jewelry, and are often used by the artisan to remove oxides and firemarks. Limes are also used to clean handsome gold ornaments. Cut one nearly in halves, and enclose the ornaments; then shut it up tightly and let it lie for a few hours. Rinse in hot water, wash in soap-suds, rinse again, and rub with chamois.

In the Door-yard.

Let the trees or shrubs that you plant in your door-yard be in proportion to its size. Large, tall-growing trees, are entirely out of place in a small enclosure; and if they are planted there, in a very few years you will be tempted to cut them down, as they will spoil the grass by their shade, and also prevent the flowers from blossoming. Therefore one must determine whether they will sacrifice these desirabilities to the large trees, for you cannot have them both in a small yard. In all cases, let the extent of your grounds determine the varieties and qualities of the trees and plants that are cultivated; and do not crowd them so closely that nothing can grow in perfection. An artistic and elaborate *parterre* will give you much more delight than a grass plot or a group of evergreens.

Directions for Whitewashing.

The return of Spring makes all housekeepers anxious to improve their surroundings, and make all things clean and sweet; and in this endeavor there is no way in which a little time and money can be better expended than in whitewashing, for it not only gives a fresh effect to both out-doors and in-doors, but it also prevents the decay of fences and outhouses, and kills the vermin which infest both poultry-houses and stables. To be sure it does not last as long as a coat of paint, but neither does it make so heavy an inroad on your purses, and as it is very cheaply prepared, and easily applied, it can be used much oftener.

The following recipe for whitewash is recommended by experts in the business:

Take half a bushel of unslacked lime, and slake it in a bucket or cask with hot water or skimmed milk. To this add one-half a pound of whiting, one pound of glue dissolved in hot water, and a peck of salt also dissolved in water.

For laying on the wash. Fix a wire across the pail so as to press off the whitewash that is not needed on the brush, as it is lifted from the pail; and, in addition to a good whitewash brush affixed to a long handle, you will need a good sized paint brush to use between the pickets on fences, and in corners.

Before whitewashing ceilings and walls, they should have the smoke, grime, and cobwebs all wiped off carefully with a broom over which a piece of thick cotton cloth has been pinned. After a little practice any one can become a skillful whitewasher. To be sure it is not easy work, for it makes the wrists and neck ache badly; but persevere in the undertaking, and you will be rewarded by the great improvement it will produce in the appearance of out-buildings, fences, etc.

Take only a small quantity at a time, upon the brush, and be careful not to let it drop on the carpets. Take care not to put on too thick a coat at the commencement, but after having gone over the ceiling once in parallel strokes, let it dry well, and then put on another coat crosswise. A good workman will dip his brush into the pail perpendicularly, and take up but little at a time, and never let a drop fall.

A whitewash that will produce a glossy appearance, and will not rub off upon every thing that comes in contact with it, can be made by using skimmed milk, boiling hot, instead of water for slacking the lime, and making it of proper thickness. It does not spread well if it is not thinly prepared.

When a ceiling has been badly blackened it is well to add a little dissolved indigo to the whitewash, as the bluish shade will serve to hide the browned surface. If other colors than white are needed, they can be made by adding different pigments to the whitewash. For stone color, use four pounds of raw umber, and two pounds of lamp-black to half a bushel of lime, and proceed as for common whitewash. For a light pink, Spanish brown can be stirred in until you have the desired shade. For a fawn color, add one pound of India red, four pounds of umber, and one pound of lamp-black, to half a bushel of lime. Chrome yellow will make a lemon-colored wash.

Calcimine.

Calcimine is a substitute for whitewash that is thought to be superior for nice work. It is made from Paris white and glue sizing. The proportion is twenty pounds of Paris white to one pound of glue, which should be dissolved in boiling water, and added to the whiting. The mixture is then diluted with water until of a creamy thickness. It requires a little practice to know how much water is needed, and it is best to try a little, and not make it too thin. Calcimine is only for hard-finish.

Some Facts About Fermentation.

The minute organisms which cause fermentation are soft and wet; moisture constitutes the greater part of their composition, and therefore, in a dry medium they cannot be formed. Applications of a mere drying process are among the most important agencies for preventing fermentation. Germs of decomposition or putrefaction may be present in fruit or vegetable substances, but if you take away the greater part of this moisture, you will make the substance incapable of decomposing. Among the agents which are desirable for that purpose, there are some which abstract the water, not in a state of vapor, but in the liquid state. For instance, if we put a piece of fresh meat in contact with salt, or by rubbing it over with salt, it will gradually absorb the water. When fruit and sugar have been boiled together, it will keep well if the pots are fastened up air tight, while hot. But if little germs from the air fall upon it, they will retain their vitality, and will soon commence to form what is called mould, which is the lowest phase of vegetable life. But if the germs in the air are shut in at a boiling point, they will be destroyed, and fermentation cannot take place.

To Make Rugs Out of Old Carpets.

No matter how faded or worn out may be the pieces of old carpeting, they can be turned to good account by first washing them, and then raveling them out, and as you do so wind it into a ball. If the colors are much faded and dulled, purchase some scarlet, blue and green yarns to mingle with, and enliven them. Then take a yard-stick, and wind the raveled yarn tightly around it, interspersing it with a little red and green all the way through; when the stick is closely covered, commence with a big needle threaded in the yarn, and sew over each loop to hold it in place; then cut it open on the outer edge. Proceed in the same way, making stickful after stickful of what looks like a narrow fringe, until your yarns are all used up, and you have a large basketful of the fringes. A piece of strong crash will answer best for a foundation of the rug, and after hemming it at each end, begin in the middle with a tuft of the brightest colored yarns, and sew the rest closely around it until the crash is completely covered with the tufted lines. It can be made of a circular or oblong shape, and if the tufts are not even, they can be sheared until they present a close surface.

These mats will be very serviceable for bed-rooms, and will wear as long as a piece of carpeting.

Home-Made Feather Dusters.

Very useful dusters for furniture, wall-corners and cornices can be made out of the feathers of barn-yard fowls.

Select the prettiest of them, and put them into a large pan, in a moderately heated oven, for a few hours, so as to heat them thoroughly, but not bake them. Then run a needle that is threaded with a strong twine through the stems, at the end of the feathered part, and pound the quills flat, with a hammer, so that they will lie closely to the handle, which can be made out of a piece of an old broom stick, whittled into grooves, if you would like a graduated brush, and then painted a bright red, or black, or brown. Or you can use the handles of worn-out hand-brushes. Cover one end of the handle with thick, hot glue, and wind the feathers, closely strung together, about the stick, commencing at the lowest end. Keep the glue-pot boiling hot, and as you wind the feathers wet the ends thoroughly with the glue, so that they will stick closely to each other and the handle. When the brush is of the size you desire, cut off the twine, and wind another piece of it tightly around the quills, gluing it firmly down. Now take a piece of scarlet, green or blue enameled cloth, cut one edge in points or small scallops; fit it to the handle, sewing up the sides, so that it will go over it easily, and cover the quills of the feathers.

Make a hole with a gimlet at the upper end of the handle, and put in a string to hang up the duster, and you will be greatly pleased with your work. If there are any worn-out window brushes, you can turn them to good use, by pulling or cutting out all the old bristles, and filling up the holes with bunches of feathers run on twine. Cut off the quill ends, and cover them with glue, and insert into the holes and fill up with glue. You can use the smaller feathers for this purpose with excellent effect.

How to Remove Stains from Clothing, Etc.

Stains upon clothing, table linen, etc., are among the troublesome happenings that disturb every household; and being caused by different substances, they require different applications, according to their various natures. As a general thing, those made by acids can be removed by alkali, of which ammonia in a diluted form is the most desirable. Alkaline stains, on the contrary, must be treated with some form of acid, such as vinegar, oxalic acid, salts of lemon, etc. Fruit and wine stains, as stated elsewhere, can be removed by immediate application of salt, which should be rubbed in with the fingers, and then washed out with boiling water. No soap should be ever used, as it fixes the color.

Milk is also a good application, but if the stains of fruit and claret are fresh, salt and boiling water will never fail to extract them. Many nice housekeepers, in the fruit season, give orders to the washerwoman to scald the table-cloths and napkins, and let them lie in the boiling water, without suds, until cool, and then they can be washed in the usual way, without any fears of stains.

Turpentine, pitch or tar can be removed by saturating the spot with sweet oil, or a little clean tallow can be dropped over it hot, and allowed to remain for several hours. Scrape it off, and if the spot is still seen, repeat the process, and afterwards rub it with spirits of wine.

Spirits of turpentine will also remove all spots of paint that have not become dried. Ink spots instantly saturated with milk and rubbed hard in it, can be removed without injury to the fabric. It can be used either sweet or sour, but the latter is preferable. If white cotton or linen becomes spotted with ink, dip it into a cup of milk, and squeeze it repeatedly, until it is effaced; rinse it out in cold water. If ink is spilled on to the carpet, cover the spots with pepper and salt, rubbing them in very hard, then brush it all up in a dust pan, and if the stains are not all removed, put a tea-spoonful of oxalic acid into a small cup of warm water, and rub it up with a piece of flannel; rinse off in cold water.

If linen or cotton become scorched in ironing, wet the places at once in hot soap-suds, and place the article in the sun until it becomes bleached. Or dip the spot into sour milk, and let it remain in it for twenty-four hours, and then wash as usual. If the scorching is not too deep, butter-milk will efface it if it is rubbed hard in it, and then laid in the sun.

Oil and grease spots on floors or carpets can be covered over with a paste made of Fuller's earth and water; and when it is thoroughly dried, brush it off, and renew the covering if the grease has not been taken out entirely.

Stains of hot water on varnished tables can be taken out by rubbing them over with a little sweet oil, and then wash it off thoroughly with a few drops of alcohol. But let the sweet oil stay on it for twenty-four hours before applying the spirits.

Ink spots on furniture can be effaced by washing them with diluted oil of vitriol—a tea-spoonful to one or two table-spoonfuls of water. Apply the acid with a bit of flannel, and when the ink is gone, polish the spot with a little oil.

To Oil the Doors, Etc.

Never allow a door to creak for want of oil, or to shut so hard as to need to be slammed to. To prevent this it is only needful to dip a feather into a little oil, occasionally, and rub every part of the hinges, handles, etc., and swing them backwards and forwards until not the least sound is to be heard. A few drops of oil will make a great difference with the comfort of the family in this respect, and the doors and walls will last much longer if they are not continually pounded and battered.

If your scissors cut hard put the feather on to the hinge, or pivot upon which they turn; and even the cutting edges can be improved by the least mite of oil being passed over them.

A Revolving Fire-Grate.

A revolving fire-grate has been invented that is said to be a great economizer of fuel. The avoidance of the usual upright draughts of air has the effect of throwing almost the whole of the heat out at the front of the grate, and also of preventing the fire from spreading amongst the coals below, and behind the central cylinder.

The combustion is so gradual that the grate, once filled, does not require to be replenished for twelve or fourteen hours, the fire burning clearly for the whole of that time, with much less attention than is the case with a common grate.

All that is needful is to occasionally apply the lever by which the grate is made to revolve, so that as the live coals become burned out, those which are not yet fully ignited can supply their places.

The cost of construction is about the same as that of an ordinary grate; and, with some very slight alterations, the principle can be applied advantageously to cooking ranges, as well as to hot-air furnaces.

Home Interests.
OUR CHILDREN.

The children are the most beautiful ornaments, and we may say also, the best safeguards of human life, since it is the children, who give to home its crowning grace, and to our hearts the incentive and reward of affectionate self-sacrifice.

They are the tender and unconscious champions of human nature, and, in its own despite, save it from confirmed and hopeless disrepute. In their innocence we see what we have lost, and may yet regain. In their confiding faith we are taught what it is that alone can compensate for our ignorance and our weakness.

In their natural and spontaneous love, we find the evidence of a possibility of the soul which may at last be triumphant over groveling hatreds. In their simplicity of taste, and its easy gratification, we discover how the best things are nearest to us, and in their facile methods of accommodating themselves to the exigencies of life, with but a temporary disturbance, we see how poor and profitless is all the fret and worry, with which we weakly combat unpleasant episodes.

The dear little philosophers! The involuntary melodists, singing all day long like the Greek grasshopper! The tender explorers whose every hour is a voyage of discovery into new Eldorados! The engaging bundles of whim and piquant caprice, and enchanting waywardness.

The naturally inspired, to whom each new moment is a fresh revelation, every sensation a surprise, every incident an event for wide-eyed wonder!

The puzzling repetitions of ourselves, loved as we were, and loving as we did, reading the books which we read, and revolting in an amusingly energetic way at the same discipline, to which, alas! not long ago we also wriggled ineffectual protest.

We go to them to peruse the first chapter of our own biography, and then, with a half feeling of pain, we look into our own hearts to read likewise the last chapters of their own.

Our Boys.

Boys require sympathy and appreciation. They will not ask for it; for a boy will abide by the way he is treated and make the best of it, but he starves for kindness and praise all the same.

It is not enough to give them food and clothes and schooling; they have an inside life that hungers to be ministered unto. As soon as they begin to think, the conflict of questions and passions begins in their souls, and their minds will question you upon various subjects. Answer their questions—do not evade them, no matter how intricate or searching they may be, for they will find an answer to them from some other source, that may not lead them up higher in the scale of existence. The way of the world with boys is a daily astonishment to us. By the majority of parents, at least, we hope that they are taught to cultivate habits of economy, and to control their appetites and passions, but there are few cases where they are kindly counseled and warned against indulging evil desires.

Mothers should obtain the confidence of their boys, so that they will come to her for aid and guidance upon every subject in life.

Yet this is rarely so, and often they will seem to have nothing in common. The mother should be the one to strengthen and uphold her boys, and to call out from them the purest and highest aspirations. She should take an interest in what they read, and ask them to read aloud to her while she sews; she should be interested in all their hopes and plans, and teach them to feel that whatever interests and excites them is also of great interest to her.

She should prove the height and depth of their nature; learn the pitfalls ready to entrap them, and make them understand that she is ever ready to counsel, and guide, and assist them in every undertaking.

In Sparta the women were put through the same gymnastic drill as the men, no matter how trying it was to their physique, so that they might produce a race of men worthy of their country.

And in the United States women need not only strength of body, but also strength of mind and soul, so that their sons may be worthy of their country— may be such

"Kings as make crowns look wan."

In a land where any man may become a ruler, it behooves the mothers to carefully guide her sons, in every phase of childhood and youth; and to leave them a legacy of confidence in the power and purity of women, which will be of more value to them in the battle of life, than all the philosophy of the schools.

Simplicity in Living.

To live simply, to master and control our expenditures, is a sore need for all classes. The influences which surround us, the habits which we fall into as a second nature, all sway us in the same direction. Every family and every class seem to have caught hold of the skirts of the one above it, and to be desperately holding on.

Well, as Mr. Goldwin Smith says, the best thing they can do is to let go; the only thing, indeed, which will give themselves any comfort, or make their lives of real use in their generation.

The moment they will do this, and begin resolutely to live without regard to what their neighbor on the right or left spends on carriages and horses, or their neighbors on the left in upholstery and dress, they will find themselves rich enough for all good purposes.

And from that moment it can no longer be said of us with truth, that we dare not trust our wits to make our houses pleasant, and so we buy ice-creams; and this most needed of all reforms is just the one which every soul of us can carry through for himself or herself.

We cannot sweep our whole streets, but every one of us can sweep our own door-step, and if we will do it quietly and regularly, anon our right and left-hand neighbors will follow, and before long the whole street will be swept.

And in this way, and by this means, can almost all these social tangles be set right.

SIMPLE LIVING! That is what the necessities of the times demand, and when we have once commenced to reform our households to this code, we shall wonder that we ever allowed ourselves to be the slaves of such customs and fashions.

Modern Comforts.

It would do those people good who are always wishing for the good old times of our ancestors, to travel back a few hundred years and see in what respects they differ so greatly. The chief feature of modern times, and one which is generally overlooked, is the adaptation of beauty and luxury to common life.

The day-laborer has a breakfast which Queen Elizabeth, in all her glory, could not have obtained; and for five or six cents he can ride to his work in an easier and more luxurious carriage than many a coach that was the pride of royalty.

Tea, coffee, sugar, vegetables, fresh meats, glass windows, white underclothing, and even the common use of soap and water are all modern luxuries. So are carpets, stoves, pictures, and all the labor-saving machines, and the comfort-producing utensils of every description; so about all our books, newspapers, magazines, and thousands of beautiful things in industrial and art life, which tend to make human existence more attractive and enjoyable.

Our Homes.

We read a good deal, now-a-days, about its being the duty of women to make home attractive to their husbands, and it is said that all the petty annoyances of daily life should be kept from them, and they should find the home in holiday attire, and the meals all ready, when they return from their business avocations.

This is all well enough if it only could be carried out, and when it is practicable there is no doubt but a good wife would make it her crowning pleasure to have everything about the house in good order, and herself and the children neatly dressed to receive the father of the family. But is there not another side to the question? And when we speak of duty, is it not also as incumbent upon the husband to make home attractive to the wife?

Yet this is a phase of the question which is not often discussed in the newspapers; and there is a tendency among men in general, to regard home as a place where the mask of politeness, which has been worn all day in their business occupations, can be cast aside, and they can show themselves in the natural man, i. e., can exhibit all their natural vices, and not restrain themselves in the least. As the head of the family they think that the ordering of its affairs devolves upon them, and there are those who incline to pay little deference to the wishes of the wife, and consult their own convenience and pleasures upon all occasions. Can there be comfort or happiness in the household where this state of affairs exists?

Can the wife love and honor the husband who does not consult her tastes or wishes, even, in the smallest matters of the family arrangements? Is she to be contemned if she takes less interest in his comforts and pleasures, and, at length, becomes alienated from such a domestic tyrant? We think the home should always be under the direct control of the wife, and that she should be allowed to order all the details connected with it; but the husband should be willing to give her aid and counsel in its affairs, and not ridicule and tease her concerning matters that seem to him too trifling to be discussed.

Then the homestead should be settled upon her, so that she can feel assured, no matter what reverses of fortune may arise, that the home which has become sanctified to her by births and deaths, and the associations of years, will be her own.

Every woman feels that this is her right, and if the husband can purchase a home, it is as much for his interest as for hers, that the deeds should be made out in her name. Then she can adorn and ornament both the house and grounds with the work of her hands, assured that its comforts and conveniences will belong to the family, and not become the property of others, without her full consent; and she would strive more heartily to make the home more attractive, as each year passed by, and to have her family appreciate its charms more highly.

Make the House Comfortable.

There are thousands of homes where the inmates are exceedingly uncomfortable, simply from inattention to little trifles. We have no patience with the housekeeper who will let the windows rattle in the casements, when a lath or two, a hammer and a few nails, and a little putty, could, with a small amount of labor, make them snug and comfortable, both in summer and winter.

We fully believe in thorough ventilation, but it should be under control, and not applied by means of cracks and crevices.

See that the outside door fits snugly. An outer portable house inclosing the most exposed door, or where the family have egress and ingress most frequently, is also a great comfort.

A damper in the stove-pipe will prevent the heat from going up the chimney, and save fuel greatly. Where coal is used, and charcoal not easily procured, a barrel of dry corn cobs will be a great addition to the kindlings. If wood is used, see that the wood-house is well filled with dry wood, finely split, for the stove, and that there are always kindlings ready for use.

A comfortable sitting-room well-lighted, and supplied with good books, and useful papers and magazines, will always make home attractive to the young folks.

Give the family good beds, and nutritious food well prepared, and pleasant evenings at home, and you will not be obliged to endure the heart-ache because they stray from the fold and enter into evil ways. For it is at home that the character should be formed, and the future usefulness of our children depends in a great degree upon the way in which their evenings are passed, as well as their days.

Fun at Home.

Don't be afraid of a little fun at home, good people, no matter if the noise is not what you were accustomed to hear in your early homes.

Don't shut up your pleasantest rooms, and keep the curtains down lest the sun should fade your carpets, and spoil your furniture. Don't shut up your hearts, either, lest a laugh should shake down some of the musty old cobwebs you have hung around it.

If you desire to make your sons seek enjoyment and happiness away from you, teach them that all mirth and joyousness must be left on the threshold when they return from school, or their various occupations. When they have once been taught to feel that their homes are only a place in which to eat, drink and sleep, the work is commenced that will probably end in their degradation and destruction. 'For young people must have fun and amusement somewhere.

It is as natural for them to dance and make merry, as it is for lambs to skip and dance in the green fields beside their sober, woolly mothers. And if they cannot find these pleasures in their homes, they will surely seek for them in questionable places.

Therefore, let us beg of you to make your homes so delightful that your children cannot be tempted to stray from them, and in their manhood and womanhood will always look back to their childhood as the happiest time of their existence.

Don't repress their buoyant spirits only so far as to prevent rudeness; half an hour's fun after tea will send them to bed happy and rosy, while it will serve to blot out the little annoyances of the day to yourselves. We pity the mother who cannot find time to play with her children, and despise the father whose chief pleasure does not consist in making them happy.

A Plea for Open Fires.

In every household there should be some arrangement for at least one open fire-place, where either wood or soft, or even hard coal can be burned, and shed a bright blaze around the room "ere the evening lamps are lighted." A fire that can not only be felt but also seen. A cheerful, bright fire, with a brilliant shovel and tongs, and fender too, is really of great influence in the delights of the home circle. Those grim, black, sulphurous flues, often filled with the stale odors of the cellar and hot-air chamber, and seething water tank, and sending upwards clouds of almost imperceptible ashes to stifle your breath, and blacken your furniture and walls, are surely one of the greatest detriments to family enjoyment and comforts.

It is very desirable, no doubt, to have your house well warmed from top to bottom, and to have no wood, coals or ashes to be carried about, soiling the carpets, and making extra work; but it has not served to bring families together, into one room, whose attractions surpassed all others on account of the cheery comfort of its fireside, but rather to throw apart the inmates of the house.

And alas! how few houses can boast of a fireside—such as our grandfathers enjoyed, and around whose cheerful blaze the sweetest associations of home ever lingered.

Don't Shut Out the Sunshine.

Seclusion from the sunshine is one of the misfortunes of civilization. No matter if it fades your elegant carpets, and your costly draperies, fasten back the blinds and draw back the curtains, and let its pure, serene rays flood every part of the house, where they can enter.

The reason that the daughters of the wealthy are so pale and delicate, is that they live an artificial life, sleeping the best part of the day, and shutting out the life-giving rays of the sun from their apartments, while if they exposed themselves to its direct rays daily, they would soon begin to show an increase of color, health and strength.

If the blue glass cure can only be brought into every day use all over the Union, it would doubtless be of the greatest benefit, because the blinds would not be closed, and the sun excluded so persistently from the apartments.

The sun-cure has been practiced in England for several years past, and there are establishments there which have acquired a wide reputation for curing those maladies in which nervous prostration is the promoting cause.

The slate, or shingled roof was removed, and glass was substituted; and the patient had a little apartment, where he could expose his body to the direct influence of the sun, by lying on a lounge, and letting it fall upon all parts of the body in turn.

Quite wonderful cures were thus effected; and very likely the blue glass discovery of General Pleasanton will give a new impetus to this method of restoring the nervous sufferer to health. But let us beg those of our readers who are well to throw open their windows to the sun, and let its health-giving rays perform their special functions, and enliven and cheer the household.

Be Faithful in Little Things.

Let us always remember that God looks in our actions, only for the motive. The world judges us by appearances; God counts for nothing that which is most dazzling to men. What He desires is a pure intention, true docility, and a sincere self-renunciation. All this is exercised more frequently, and in a way that tries us more severely on common than on great occasions, and sometimes we cling more tenaciously to a trifle than to a great interest; and it would give no more pain to relinquish an amusement, than to bestow a great sum in charity. We are more easily led away by little things, because we believe them more innocent, and imagine that we are less attached to them; nevertheless, when God deprives us of them, we soon discover, from the pain of privation, how excessive and inexcusable was our attachment to them. The sincerity of our piety is, also, impeached, by the neglect of minor duties. What probability is there that we should not hesitate to make great sacrifices, when we shrink from slight ones?

But what is most dangerous to the mind is the habit it acquires of unfaithfulness. True love to God thinks nothing small. All that can please or displease Him is great. It does not produce constraint and weak scruples, but it places no limits to its fidelity; it acts with simplicity, and, as it is not embarrassed with things that God has not commanded, it never hesitates a moment about what He does command, whether it be great or small.—*Fenelon.*

Comfort in Sleeping-Rooms.

Good ventilation is the chief requisite in every sleeping-room; and yet it is a condition that is not always attained to, even in the houses of the rich; while in the country, where pure air ought surely to be found, if anywhere, visitors shrug their shoulders at the vitiated atmosphere that abounds in the "best rooms."

And it is true that you rarely find, in the country, a large old-fashioned cham-her redolent with the sweetness that sunshine and fresh air only can produce. To be sure, the room may be well-furnished with articles of refinement, etc., but purity of atmosphere, its chief essential, and seemingly the cheapest thing in the world, will not be often met with.

There is a dampness and mouldiness that infects the air of unused chambers in hundreds of well-furnished houses, that is simply intolerable to those who are accustomed to fresh and clean apartments.

When chambers are swept, it is a good plan, every two or three weeks, to wipe the dust from the carpets with a dampened cloth or mop, and always to dust the furniture with a damp cloth, so as not to throw the dust upon some other article, but wipe it up. The dust of bedrooms is said to abound in exhalations of the body, thrown off upon the bedclothing; and the mouth should always be kept tightly closed while making the beds, so as not to inhale them.

Moderately warmed sleeping-rooms are a great addition to personal comfort, and there is no surer avenue to the grave, than that of cold beds and cold chambers. Neuralgia, pneumonia, and consumption itself, can often be traced to the comfortless room in which delicate girls are forced to sleep. The most economical way of warming the upper part of the house is by a large coal or wood stove placed in the hall with pipes running into each chamber; and, with a very small amount of fuel, the rooms will all be made comfortable. Soap-stone stoves, thus arranged, are quite as desirable for heating purposes, as hot air furnaces, while they will not consume as much fuel, and they will keep the air as soft as if heated by steam.

The porcelain stoves of the Germans and Russians are also superior to most of our methods of warming houses, and they could be imitated in this country with great benefit. The soap-stone stoves, however, are almost as desirable, and every year they gain in popularity, and are rapidly superseding the cast-iron stoves, which are considered unhealthy from the poisonous gas generated from them.

A vase of water with a little charcoal in it, to keep it pure, should always be kept upon the stove; and both it and the charcoal should be changed weekly.

To ventilate a chamber the lower and upper part of the sashes should be opened, so that the fresh air can enter below, and the foul air find egress at the top.

In well warmed sleeping-rooms, it is a good plan to insert a sheet of zinc, well perforated with holes in the upper part of the sash, and thus give the foul air a good opportunity to escape.

Of late years the doctors have had a great deal to say against valances and curtains to beds, so that they have been nearly discarded from common use. Habit and association, however, have such strong hold upon us all, that those of us who passed the nights of our youth under the curtains of a four-poster will still consider them superior in coziness, warmth and seclusion, to any modern style of bedstead.

It can easily be understood that the almost entire exclusion of fresh air must be injurious; but it must be admitted that a bedstead does look bare and comfortless when entirely denuded of drapery. We must therefore content ourselves with a compromise, and purchase a canopy for the head of the bedstead.

There has also been a discussion of late years upon the healthful merits of iron and brass or woods. But we incline to take up the cudgels in favor of the latter, and declare that ornament an iron one as you will, decorate it with gilding or inlay it with brass, it can never equal the beauty of beautifully painted or grained wood.

For places where crowds do congregate, the iron ones may possess the best qualifications on account of their cleanliness, and their being less likely to retain infection; but it seems to us that they never can look as comfortable.

The most luxurious arrangement for a bed is to lay a horse-hair mattress on the top of a spring mattress. To be sure the latter is a costly appurtenance compared with an under bed of "excelsior" or straw. Yet it is *par excellence* preferable to them. It is very poor economy to purchase poor beds; they must be paid for well in the beginning, and then they will last many years, and can be made over as good as new, whenever they become soiled.

One rule should be invariable with every good housekeeper, viz., that the guest-chamber's bed should never be made up with sheets and blankets until needed for visitors. Cover it with a bed-spread to keep the beds from dust, but keep the blankets and sheets in boxes or drawers, and put them on only when required. A sun-wholesome, fresh, sweet room, with a dry bed and plenty of well-aired bedclothes, is within the means of the poorest to give their visitors.

It should be the pride of every housekeeper to possess clean, sweet beds, and to keep them in such a condition that they can be quickly prepared for use. Good pillows are also very essential to good sleep. And it is poor economy to purchase old ones, but far better to buy new feathers, and ticking, and make the pillows in the house.

If you have old pillows whose feathers need renovating, put them on the grass the first rainy day, and let them get well wetted. Turn them on the other side until the tick is washed clean. Then take them from the grass, and pin to the clothes-line, or hang on a pole to dry, shaking them up occasionally. When thoroughly dried beat with a stick for ten minutes; and you will have pillows as good as new.

All the pieces of furniture in a room should correspond in color, *i. e.*, be of the same kind of natural or painted woods. Painted furniture can be purchased very cheaply, and it is made in pleasing shapes. Sets that are painted of some light tint with a narrow gilt band, or a relief of pink, blue, green or garnet have a very good effect, and can be repainted at any time.

In arranging the furniture, take care to place the bed so that it is not opposite a window, for the light falling upon the face is often injurious to the eyes. But if it cannot be avoided, it is a good plan to have double shades, the outer one being of green or blue, and the inner one white. Or dark glazed cambric can be pinned to the white curtains.

A prettily draped dressing table is one of the most effective objects in a bedroom if its appointments are kept neat and natty. If tastefully made, with dotted muslin and colored cambrics, and ornamented with ribbons, it always gives good satisfaction, until it must be dismantled for the laundry. A half circular table of common pine, thus covered, and a good sized mirror suspended over it, and prettily draped, can be procured at a slight expense from any furnishing store.

Home Culture.

This is a text from which many sermons are written now-a-days, not only for the pulpit, but also for the newspaper and magazine, and it surely does not come amiss to write upon it for "*Scraps for the Household.*"

So let us beg of our lady readers to cultivate a taste for literature in all its branches, to learn to appreciate a fine poem, essay, and historical work, as well as to enjoy the last sensation novel.

Do not let the gentlemen of the household take possession of the cosy library, but place your chair and foot-stool, and work-stand there, and share its privileges; and ask that some interesting book, magazine or paper may be read aloud, and thus beguile the monotony of the needle. By this means you can gather up many pearls of wisdom, while you busily ply the needle, or the crochet hook.

Practice reading aloud yourselves, for it is one of the best and also the rarest accomplishment that women can possess, while it is also one of the most charming pastimes for the family circle. A high-toned literary taste is considered most needful for a true lady; and no one should allow her time to be so occupied that she cannot become acquainted with English classics, the poets, dramatists, essayists, novelists, etc., as well as with the current magazine literature of the day. Such studies will serve to make your mind rich and ripe, and to take away all flippancy and pedantry.

It is one of the most desirable exercise of women's rights, to insist upon sharing the literary pursuits of the sterner sex, and to show yourselves capable of understanding all things connected with them.

A part of every twenty-four hours should be especially set apart for home culture, and if you do not feel a great interest in the pursuit at the first, you will find that it will increase daily, and it will prevent you from degenerating into nothing but a housekeeper who does not possess a soul above preserves or pickles, or into a gossip whose chief occupation consists in collecting stories about her neighbors, and into relating them from house to house.

It will give you richness and breadth of thought, and also provide you with something to talk about besides fashions, and the annoyances of your household; for although a chat upon dress and a little pleasant gossip may not come amiss in a friendly visit, yet when one makes them the chief topics of conversation on all occasions, it shows how very small is the pivot upon which the mind turns. Moreover, if you thus cultivate your own minds, you will be able to give your children a higher standard of excellence, and can teach them that books are often far better companions than those who talk and run about.

And a cultivated intellect is never at loss for companionship of the highest order, while the heavens above us, the earth beneath us, and the waters, all pay tribute to it. Astronomy, geology, and all animated nature, open their stores of treasures to those who will seek them, and there is not a moment of our waking existence but can be employed in learning something that is both of use and interest. A foreign language can be learned in the few minutes that one waits for the summons to dinner. In "*Lord Macauley's Life and Letters*," one reads with amazement of his wondrous powers of devouring knowledge, and yet, if you would only commence the practice in good earnest, you will be surprised at your own powers of voracity in the pursuit.

The Grumbler.

As there are few households wherein the spirit of grumbling doth not dwell, it may not be out of place in a scrap-book prepared for the family, to quote the following from the graphic pen of the well-known H. H.:

"Oh, who can describe him?"

There is no language that can do justice to him, no supernatural foresight which can predict where his next thrust will fall, from what unsuspected corner he will send his next arrow.

Like death, he has all seasons for his own; his ingenuity is infernal. Whoever tries to forestall or appease him, might better be at work in Augean stables; because, after all, we must admit that the facts of life are on his side. It is not intended that we shall be very comfortable here. There is a terrible amount of total depravity in animate and inanimate things!

From morning till night there is not an hour without its cross to carry. The weather thwarts us; servants, landlords, drivers, washerwomen and bosom friends misbehave; clothes don't fit; teeth will ache; stomachs will get out of order; newspapers are stupid; and children make too much noise.

If there are not big troubles there are little ones. If they are not in sight, they are hiding. I have wondered whether the happiest mortal could point to one single moment, and say:

"At that moment there was nothing in my life which I would have had changed."

I think not. In argument, therefore, the grumbler has the best of it. It is more than probable that things are just as he says.

But why say it? Why make four miseries out of three?

If the three be unbearable, so much the worse. If he is uncomfortable it is a pity; we are sorry, but we can't change the course of nature. We shall soon have our own little turn of torments, and we do not wish to be worn out before it comes, by having to listen to his; probably, too, the very things of which he complains, are pressing just as heavily on us as on him.

Suppose every one did as he does. Imagine, for instance, a course of grumble from ten persons at breakfast table, all saying at once, or immediately after each other :

"This coffee is not fit to drink. Really, the attendance at this house is insufferably poor."

I have sometimes wished to try the homeopathic treatment, "*similia similibus curantur,*" in a bad case of grumble. It seems as if it might work a cure.

If you lose your temper with the grumbler, and turn upon him suddenly, saying, "Oh, do not spoil all our pleasure! Do make the best of things, or at least keep quiet." See how aggrieved he is; how unjust he thinks you are to "make a personal matter of it." "You do not, surely, suppose I think you are responsible for it, do you," he asks, with a lofty air of astonishment at your unreasonable sensitiveness.

Of course we do not suppose he thinks we are to blame; we do not take him to be a fool as well as a grumbler. But he speaks to us, at us, before us, about the cause of his discomfort, whatever it may be, precisely as he would if we were to blame, and that is the one thing which makes his grumbling so insufferable. But this he can never be made to see. And the worst of it is that grumbling is contagious. If we live with him, we shall, sooner or later, in spite of our dislike of his ways, fall into them.

There is no help for this. I have seen it again and again. I have caught it myself. One grumbler in a family is as pestilential a thing as a diseased animal in a herd; if he be not shut up or killed, the herd is lost.

Appropriateness of Pictures.

Pictures are always charming additions to our surroundings, but there is a certain fitness belonging to them, that does not seem to be understood by every owner of paintings.

For instance, a battle scene does not seem appropriate for a parlor or sleeping-room, and we cannot see the propriety of adorning a sick chamber with a floral cross or wreath taken from a casket; as it is not always a narcotic to a sick person to be reminded that death is close at hand.

And we know of but few localities where skulls and cross bones are not out of place. They might possess significance in a druggist's store, beside his pills and poisons, but surely not in another place, unless it is in a phrenologist's apartment, or a physician's office.

Give us magnificent landscapes for our parlors, landscapes that will thrill us with joyousness, and inspire us with noble thoughts every time we cast our eyes upon them.

In our dining rooms, let us collect handsome portraits, and lovely representations of flowers and fruits, game, etc., and in our sleeping apartments let us hang the lovely faces of children, and of youths' faces that will give us pleasing thoughts as we hover on the borders of nod land.

Let us hang in the sick room peaceful landscapes of sun-lit valleys, with only shadow sufficient to give them an appearance of rest and peace; or happy glimpses of a clear, still bit of water, with a peaceful, quiet shore.

Such pictures are conducive to the peace of the soul, are restful to the storm-tossed spirit, and do not distract and annoy a sufferer. Painful representations are out of place in the household, and are rarely to be seen where the spirit of peace abides.

A Hint to Mothers.

It is a wise thing to send the babies into the open air, if possible, every day, but it is exceedingly needful to confide them to competent hands, and not allow a scatter-brained young girl, in whose hands you would not trust your cut-glass dishes, to take out the child whom you cherish as the dearest possession life holds for you; and if you do this you may be sure that the little tender darling will be bounced into and over gutters, thumped over crossings at headlong speed, and tossed about and wearied out, until it receives more harm than good from its airing.

Every observant person, who walks in the streets of town or city, will tell you how roughly and even crossly, the little nurse girls handle their charges, and how they often feel obliged to speak to them words of caution concerning the way in which they treat the children.

It is perfectly easy to guide a child's carriage over a gutter without a jar, but it is rarely done by a servant, and the little ones are jerked and bumped along in this wearisome style, sometimes for hours without change of position, until they become quite exhausted; and very serious evils have been the result in several cases that have come to our knowledge.

Mothers should make it their pleasure to go out with their children, and show the nurses exactly how to guide the carriages, and also to see that they do not take them into the thoroughfares of the town, but select some open, pleasant street, where the passers by are not numerous; and if they cannot always go out themselves, they should if possible, send another child, or in some way be assured that their commands are obeyed; and that the baby receives healthful air and exercise.

Very young babies should always be carried out in the arms, as the jar of the pavements is not desirable for them; and many spinal diseases have been produced by the baby-carriages of the day.

HOUSEHOLD HINTS AND RECIPES.

A Good Plan for a Kitchen.

A kitchen should be so situated that it will have the full morning sun to light it up brightly, and also be shaded from it at noon-day; and the windows should be large, and easily opened, both from the top and bottom, so as to secure good ventilation. And to fully insure this, it is an excellent idea to have a large circular device, like an old fashioned sounding board, suspended over the cooking stove, with a hole in the center, and a tube or pipe leading into the chimney, to carry off the savory odors, which the process of cooking generally diffuses all over the house. For however agreeable the odors may be in the kitchen, they are especially annoying to delicate olfactories in the parlor, when they have become stale and flat.

A large sink, with handsome copper basins and suitable implements for washing dishes, and a wooden drainer attached to it, is indispensable. And adjustable pipes leading from the hot and cold water tanks, should be attached to it.

Various cupboards and closets can also be built into or attached to the walls, which will not only be very convenient, but can also be made decorative. In the pantry there should be a special closet for the flour barrel, and one for the sugar barrel with covers attached by hinges, and a small chest of drawers should be built up at one side, with tiny partitions for all kinds of spices, and condiments used in cooking, and each one should be labeled, so that at a glance the cook can see what she needs, without looking through numerous boxes for the articles.

Cookery is rapidly becoming a complicated art, and the cook needs to have all her utensils and essentials so arranged that they can be obtained in a moment.

"*A place for everything, and everything in its place,*" is a maxim that applies particularly to the kitchen department.

The Art of Color.

There are comparatively very few ladies who really comprehend the law of colors, as applied to their toilettes and apartments. Many a lady, although she may be robed in the costliest materials, and considers herself a mirror of fashion, in the cut of her garments, will yet lack the indescribable something which should harmonize the whole, and give to it an air of elegance and grace; and the educated eye will observe this want at once, and will know that the hues of her costume are not in exact harmony. And a lady who is dressed in simple black cashmere, with spotless lingerie, and merely a knot of blue or crimson ribbon at her throat, will often be the best dressed of the two.

There are those who will wear a ruby colored dress, with bows of like ribbon, and wonder why the effect is not pleasing, when all the fashion folks say that red and blue are excellent contrasts. If she had selected blue for the prevailing hue, and contrasted it with ruby colored ribbons, she would not have had reason to deplore its bad effect; and it should always be borne in mind, that if masses of color are not distributed in equal, or nearly equal proportions, as in plaids or stripes, the soberer hue should always be the predominant color; but it should be relieved by a dash of brightness. A dress of the dark, rich crimson shade, called maroon color, will be well relieved by knots or bows of bright blue, but that is not a flaming red.

A little knowledge of the harmony of colors is not to be disregarded by any lady, but is a needful part of her education; and will prove of great assistance in teaching her not only to dress tastefully, but also to arrange her rooms effectively. Yet bright colors should always be sparingly employed.

Hints upon House-Linen.

In portioning out the money for purchasing house furniture, etc., a good share should be laid aside for the house-linen, which is so essential a part of housekeeping. Its several items will form a lengthy list, and, like kitchen utensils, and other apparently insignificant but needful adjuncts of a house, a good many dollars can be consumed in their purchase, and there will be but little to show in comparison with the amount of the outlay, excepting to those who comprehend the value of fine damask. And there are many ladies who take more pride in their elegant and costly table linen, chamber towels, sheets, etc., than in the silver and glass that make so much handsomer a show. Yet the exhibition of it in dining-room and bed-room, is considered by many as a great test of the wealth of the housekeeper, and her position in society.

To those who do not know the merits and demerits of double and single damask, and who take no thought concerning the fineness of their sheets, nor the width of their hems, nor the breadth of the pillows and their cases, nor the beauty of their bed-spreads, nor the softness and thickness of their blankets; all these things will seem of minor importance. Our great grandmothers frequently spun their own linen sheets, and towels, and wove their blankets, and pieced up and quilted their bed-quilts, and delighted to exhibit their riches stored away in chests and presses, to the wondering eyes of their grandchildren, and lovingly to finger the sheets and towels that they had labored so constantly to possess. And we hardly believe that they would have permitted a cotton sheet to intrude into their linen presses, although they are in such general use at present. We will give a list of the items of house linen that are needed in every household.

Table-cloths, napkins, tray-cloths and doilies, kitchen table-cloths, glass, tea, knife, and dish cloths; roller towels and dusters; sheets, bolster and pillow-cases, pillow-shams, sheets and shams, chamber towels and toilet covers; and bed-spreads, both thick and thin. The cost of table-linen varies with the price of linen. Single damask is not more than half the cost of double damask, the latter, however, will wear twice as long as the former, as it has much more substance, and the patterns are shown in stronger relief. Spots and sprigs are less expensive than those which have a centre design and a border; and table-linen is always cheaper if purchased by the yard, than by the single cloth, with a complete pattern.

To show you how expensive handsome table-linen is, we quote from an English magazine the price of a double damask table-cloth from seven to eight yards in length at $50; and table napkins to match, would be from $11.00 to $12.00 per dozen. Passing through our custom-house would add considerably to their price. It is now the fashion to have table-napkins larger than formerly. The medium size is, however, the most convenient, 26 by 30 inches; and the prices would vary from $5.00 to $10.00 per dozen, according to the patterns, as the beauty of the design adds largely to the price. Tray-cloths and bureau-cloths are usually of uniform size, 34 by 43 inches, and they range in price according to quality and pattern. The small fringed napkins are often used at the tea-table, and cost from 75 cents to $4.00 or $5.00 per dozen.

When you desire to purchase linen, be sure that you can depend upon the word of the seller, and see that no cotton is intermixed with the linen, for it never will look smooth and glossy after it is washed if it is. For kitchen and nursery table-cloths, a strong half-bleached linen is sold by the yard that always gives good satisfaction, if a good quality is purchased.

Kitchen towels can be made of Russia crash or huckaback, and the best size is 23 by 35 inches; but often the crash comes much narrower. White loom towels can also be purchased at a small cost that will prove serviceable. Torfar towels are excellent for rough usage.

For roller towels the white or mixed crash and the huckaback are the best, and they should be made two yards and a half in length. Buy a piece of the crash and cut it into towels, sewing it firmly together.

Dusters are often a nuisance to housekeepers, as they are so liable to be lost or thrown away by careless house-maids, instead of being carefully washed, and used until they are wanted. Very serviceable ones are woven in blue and white mixed cotton, with a fuzzy center that wipes up the dust readily, and they can be purchased for twenty-five cents each. Colored calicoes that can be purchased for five or six cents per yard, make excellent dusters, if torn up in yard lengths and hemmed on the machine.

Dish-cloths are also a bother to neat housewives, for cooks are so apt to let them become filthy, and to use one cloth for everything. They can be made out of worn-out napkins by folding them in quarters and quilting them together loosely. They can also be bought, woven loosely in unbleached cotton, for six cents a piece, and they are far better than rags.

Iron dish or pot-cloths are a late invention that will prove of great service to the cook in saving her fingers, as with their aid a saucepan or iron pot can be scrubbed clean in a few minutes.

Sheets are the most important item in bed-room linen, and for ordinary use they should not be made of either thin or too fine linen, but that which is firm and heavy.

The two and a half width is the best for double beds; and the sheets should be cut in three yards length, and the hems of the upper edges should be four inches in width, the lower two inches. Cotton sheets of the same width and length are far preferable to those of yard and a quarter or one yard width cotton, which must be sewed together in the middle. Our grandmothers preferred that width because they were accustomed to over-seam, and thought that when the sheets were worn in the center, they could be more easily turned, but the thrifty housewife can cut her sheets through the center when it becomes thin, and sew up the selvages, and hem the edges of them with more ease than she can rip out the over-seaming and sew it up again, if she has a machine to do her bidding. Pillow-cases are made of both fine linen and cotton, but we must confess that our preferences are for the former, especially in Summer.

Square pillow-cases are made of yard wide linen or cotton, and hemmed with four inch hems to match the sheets. If both sheets and pillow-cases are marked with the initials in satin stitch, or even with braid work, it gives them a handsome finish.

Pillow-shams and sheet-shams are indispensable accessories to every bed-room, and can be made of fine linen or cambric, lace or muslin, in figures or patterns. They are embroidered in satin stitch or with braid, and trimmed with insertions and edgings; but if of lace they are mostly lined with pink or blue silk, or paper cambric can be substituted.

They will add greatly to the pleasing appearance of the bed-room, while they also protect the pillows and sheets from all particles of dust.

Chamber towels are now manufactured of great beauty, in various patterns, with open worked and lace borders, or they can be procured by the piece, and cut to the desired lengths and hemmed on the edges. They should be at least 38 or 48 inches in length. Huckaback towels of all degrees of fineness can be purchased with damask borders and wide-fringes; and for those who desire soft towels, linen diaper can be obtained, but they so soon become dampened that they are of little service excepting for the hands.

Toilette covers are woven in great varieties, but they can be made at home to give quite as good satisfaction. You can purchase a thick or thin material; if the latter, they should be lined with pink or blue cambric, and trimmed with lace edgings. If thick Marseilles or dimity is selected, trim them with a looped or crocheted figure. They should be cut to fit the bureaus or tables.

White Marseilles quilts, figured on both sides, are very handsome for winter bed-spreads, and they can be purchased for $3 to $10, according to the beauty of the pattern.

The cotton honey-comb bed-spreads are much lighter and cheaper, and those with pink or blue stripes at the sides are very effective when used with pillow and sheet-shams lined with the same color.

Knitted bed-spreads are quite the fashion now, and as some of the patterns are made in tiny triangles, they are not cumbersome to knit, but really give pleasing occupation to many elderly ladies.

Blankets, although not included in house-linen, are still so closely connected with it that a few words upon them may not be amiss.

The most expensive are in the end the cheapest, and the low price of wool the past year has brought them within the reach of many households.

Those that measure two and three quarters by three and a quarter yards are not too large for double beds. White blankets with scarlet or blue borders are the most desirable. Within a year or so scarlet blankets have been imported from England, but they are more expensive than the white.

The blankets that are manufactured in California have also been highly praised, and are very soft and warm. A pair of thick, soft, fine blankets are really of greater warmth than two pairs that are not so thick, and are made of coarser wool.

Simple Directions for Shirt Making.

If possible procure a pattern from a tailor, cut by exact measure; if this is not obtainable, take an old shirt that has given satisfaction in every particular, and rip it to pieces, and cut another by it *exactly;* then baste it up and try it on. "Try it on?" repeats the head of the household.

"Yes," we reply, "try it on if you desire to have a perfect fit, for without such a precaution your seamstress cannot be sure that the neck fits well, and the sleeves are the right length, and the whole garment well adjusted. And you well know that if the shirt fails to suit you, you will not fail to announce the fact frequently."

After it has been pinned in here, and basted up there, take it off, and rip it to pieces, and cut a pattern of it, allowing for the seams and hems.

Perhaps you may think this makes a great deal of trouble, but you will not find it as much as to hear your husband or sons grumble about a badly fitting shirt. Few seamstresses are now obliged to make bosoms, as they can be purchased for but little more than the linen would cost. But let us beg of you to buy the finest and firmest of linen, because one such bosom will outlast two cheap ones, and the finest ones will always do up the best. It is a great mistake to make shirts out of poor cotton or linen, for the work is just the same, no matter how coarse the fabric, and the dearest cotton will be much the cheapest in the end, because one good shirt will outlast two coarse ones.

Putting in the bosom is the first part of the work to be accomplished. To do this, double the front of the shirt in the middle, and also double the bosom in the same way, and place it exactly square upon the shirt. Then cut out a piece one inch wider than the bosom, and half an inch shorter.

Unfold shirt and bosom, and commence at the top of each side and baste the bosom down to the bottom. Then lay a double plait of the shirt, directly in the middle of the bottom of the bosom. Stitch the sides, and across the bottom, and then turn the bosom on the wrong side, and hem it down, it being left half an inch longer than the shirt for this purpose, and it will save the sewing of a piece of tape across it. The reason that a plait is made at the bottom of the bosom is that the front of the shirt should be narrower. The backs should always be a little wider than the fronts, to give enough room for the shoulders and arms. If both sides are of the same width, the bosom will swell out beyond the vest, as is sometimes seen in ill-fitting shirts.

Line the back of the shirt the whole length of the armholes. Face a strip around the fronts of the sleeves; or better still, if you use a yoke for the neck, cut the sleeves an inch too long, and stitch them in with an inch seam; then baste it down on the shirt all around, and stitch it. It makes as strong a facing as the old way of making it with separate facings.

The quickest and easiest way to do the seams by machine is the double fell. Sew up the shirt or sleeves upon the right side, trim off the seam closely, turn and sew up again on the wrong side, and your seam is made very strong.

The flaps can be quickly hemmed with a hemmer, and the wristbands and neck bindings added. The collars should always be made separately, as they never can fit as well if attached to the shirt.

It is much the style now to make shirts to button behind; in that case the bosom is put in whole, the plait laid in the same way, and the back either fitted into a yoke or made sack shape.

Such a shirt recommends itself to all those who do not possess mothers or sisters who will keep the buttons always in repair.

Going to Housekeeping.

A little money will go a long way now in furnishing a house, and it is generally found to be much better economy for a newly married couple to keep house, than to board. "The Lord setteth the solitary in families," and hotels and boarding-houses can never give to any one the solid happiness of "HOME." A home of one's own, where your own tastes and your own interests are of the chief importance, is a delight that words fail to portray.

To be sure, many are forced to ask the question: "How can we afford the expense of house rent and furnishing in these hard times?" But, if you can afford to board, you can also afford to keep house, especially if your wife has been trained to habits of housewifery, as she should have been, by a judicious mother who must fully understand their importance.

It is the first step which costs; but if you can afford to purchase only the needful articles for a sitting-room, dining-room, bed-room and kitchen, and do not sigh for what you can not obtain, without pledging your credit beyond redemption—you will not find the outlay to be so very large.

Make your house as handsome as your means will allow; if you can not have Brussels carpets, buy ingrain, or matting, and spread a few rugs over it.

"Furnish the kitchen and bed-room comfortably, and pinch in other things," was the advice of an excellent housekeeper to a bride. And a good cooking-stove is one of the first requisites—*an indispensable article*. To be sure, it is a costly article; but you can often procure a second-hand one, that is just as good as new, for a third of the cost of a new one, and it will be quite as serviceable for you. The furniture for it must be carefully selected, and you will need a tea-kettle, soup-pot, frying-pan, three sizes of saucepans, a dripping-pan, for roasting meat, four bread-pans, a roll-pan, coffee-pot, tea-pot, half a dozen iron spoons, of various sizes, a skimmer, gravy-strainer, colander, pie-pans, patty-pans, egg-beater, half a dozen knives and forks, a dozen kitchen plates, and the same number of cups and saucers, and nutmeg and bread graters. $12.00 or $13.00 will probably purchase these necessities, and with them a great deal of nice cookery can be accomplished. Of course, the furnishing stores will offer you many more so-called "necessities," but, with a few additions, the best of cooks should be content with this supply. But, if you have the money, by all means select some of the novelties for kitchen use, as there are many really useful articles now manufactured. For kitchen furniture, you will need a large white-wood table with two drawers, three chairs, and a rocking-chair. Also, a skirt-board, shirt-board and flat-irons; and, if there are not stationary tubs, two wash-tubs, and washboard and wringer.

A very little furniture will make the bed-room comfortable, but be sure to purchase good bedding, for a bed will last a life-time, if made over when it is soiled. An upholstered copper spring-bed is the best, and, if you cannot afford a hair mattrass, purchase three or four, or more, coarse soft blankets, and tack them together. Then cover them with unbleached cotton, or ticking, and you will have a far better bed than "excelsior" or straw mattrasses can make. Very nice bed-room furniture can be picked up, here and there, at the auctions of private families, or at auction stores; but it needs an experienced hand to buy at the latter.

Clarence Cook, who has written upon *House Furnishing* in *Scribner's Monthly*, advises young housekeepers to purchase their furniture in small lots or single pieces, so that they may not furnish their houses in a set pattern, but desire to exercise some originality; and to banish from their minds the idea that everything should be *en suite*. That the front parlor must match the back one, exactly, in the color of the upholstering; that one side of a chimney pier must just reflect the other; that there must always be a middle and sides, and so forth, and so on—laws which are Medean and Persian laws to the tradesmen and conservative, safe, respectable upholsterers; but they are not laws but we can transgress, if we only possess the courage to do so.

A lady of taste can fit up pretty and convenient articles for the bed-rooms, out of chintz, *cretonne*, and shoe or soap boxes, and, with a bureau, washstand, bedstead and two chairs and a rocker, she need not suffer for comfortable surroundings.

The dining-room will be more appropriate for its use, if it is not crowded with furniture. A good extension table of chestnut, oak, or black walnut, with half a dozen chairs to match, are essential, but a table with a red cover can do duty for a *buffet*, or side-board, if your means do not justify the purchase of the handsomer article. We should prefer to go without it, and purchase some fine engravings, well-framed, for the hall, parlor and dining-room, and wait until the length of the purse would admit of its possession.

The parlor, or sitting-room, can be left to the last in furnishing a home for mere comfort; because, if you commence with it, and expend the greater portion of your money in an expensive carpet, and a costly upholstered set of furniture, and leave the other rooms bare of various necessities, as well as comforts, though you may take a great deal of pride in exhibiting the fineries of the parlor to your visitors, yet neither husband nor wife can take half as much comfort in it, as in well-arranged living-rooms.

Indeed, we would recommend our young friends to sacrifice the parlor entirely, if they must scrimp the dining-room, bed-room and kitchen, in order to furnish it. A carpet can be laid upon the floor, and a couch table, and chairs added as convenient; then pretty *bric-a-brac* can be added, as time permits. But fill up the windows with brightly blooming plants, and twine vines over the casements, and you will give your rooms an air of refinement.

Hints upon Moving.

Take ample time to prepare your household goods, and do not allow yourself to be so hurried that you are in danger of becoming completely exhausted when the deed is done. With plenty of assistance, a fortnight will not give you any time to spare; and do not commence to take up the carpets in the rooms that are daily occupied, until you are ready to leave them, for bare floors will make the house so comfortless.

Procure all the boxes and clean barrels that are needful to pack away such fragile articles as china, glass-ware, ornaments, etc., and do each article up in paper, and dampen the hay or straw that they are packed in, unless they are going to remain packed for a long time, and there is danger of its becoming musty.

Large books can be tied together with stout twine and placed in baskets, or packed in boxes; but do not take large boxes for this purpose, as books are very heavy to handle. All large pictures should be tied in couples, face to face, with soft napkins and towels, or papers laid between them, and rolls of soft paper put in at the corners to prevent them from becoming defaced.

Wrap the pictures up in large quilts, or put them in the bedding, or roll carpets about them.

It is an excellent plan to take up the carpet in the parlor that is the least used, and to clear the room, then bring down many articles from the chambers, and pack them in that room. A good sized parlor will hold the furniture of three common rooms, and those rooms can be cleaned, and left in good order.

If you can induce the occupant of the house into which you are to move (if you are not leaving the town) to do the same, then you can have the carpet put down in those rooms, and the furniture carried there, before they leave the house, for if they will give you the keys your articles need not be molested.

Before you move, prepare a large lunch basket with all needful articles for a good meal; for it is truly deplorable to have to endure all the discomforts of moving without the assistance of tempting food. The inner man must be fortified with something nice when chaos reigns supreme on all sides of you.

Put into the basket matches, towels, napkins, knives, forks, sugar, tea, and bread and butter, and a tea-pot, as well as some toothsome cold meats and pickles for a relish. To be sure a good meal can be ordered in a city from a neighboring restaurant, but in most families a little attention to economy is required, and such a meal is often costly. Some pickled oysters will go well with the bread and butter, and ham sandwiches are always welcome. See that the coal hod is carried full of coal, and that kindlings also are ready, unless you have already had the coal bins filled, and the barrels of kindlings supplied. Of course competent housekeepers, who are accustomed to exercise forethought upon all subjects, will not need to be reminded of these trifles, which after all are so important to one's comfort. But we know that there are many housewives who are not able to comprehend their necessities until deprived of them.

Dr. Benjamin Franklin said that "three removes are as bad as one fire," and many persons can fully understand the truth of the remark; and when one understands how much it costs for cartage, and how liable are breakages and all sorts of disasters; and how exceedingly wearing such flittings are, not only to the person but to soul and mind, it is surprising that the custom of moving yearly could ever take possession of housekeepers. Far better to live in the country than to live where such toils and moils are the fashion.

How to Lay Carpets.

One of the greatest drawbacks in moving, is the loss and annoyance in cutting over and refitting old carpets to new rooms; and it is always best to sell the carpets and purchase new ones, if it can be done to good advantage; of course we would not recommend you to sell them at a decided loss.

Carpet men are so used to the work, and it really is so hard and troublesome for raw-hands to attempt it, and the work is so apt to be badly done by them, that it is better to call in their aid, if it can be obtained, and save the expense in other ways.

Carpets require a great deal of stretching and fitting to lie smoothly on the floors. The first thing to be done is to clear the room of all furniture that can be removed, and then place the carpet as the breadths were cut.

Then begin at one corner, and nail down one side of the cut ends of the breadths, never on the selvage side. When that is done, stretch the selvage along as far as possible, and nail it so that it will not be too loose, nor yet too much stretched.

Nail both selvages, and then commence in the middle and pull up the breadths of the fourth side. Here the greatest amount of strength is needed to make it lie smoothly, and it should be done by men, as few women possess the requisite power to do it well; and if the carpet is not firmly laid down, it will not wear well, and will never have a tidy appearance.

When heavy carpets have once been laid properly, they can remain so for several years; if they are properly cared for, and are wiped over with a cloth dipped in strong alum water every spring, it destroys the eggs of the moth.

Why Girls should be Taught to Keep House.

Many articles have been written upon the moral obligations that should induce our girls to desire to learn to be good housekeepers; but their arguments really possess little influence, and are sometimes quite distasteful to their minds, for many of them do not relish to be told that their chief duty should be sought in that line.

Therefore a wise mother will strive to make the task attractive; and then another view is taken of it. It is now becoming quite the fashion for young ladies to give parties, in which the entertainments have been chiefly prepared by their own fair hands, and the preparations of the various dainties will doubtless give them much pleasure and satisfaction; for it will show them how agreeable the work can be made, and their energies will be stimulated, and a desire created in them to become mistresses of the fine art of cookery, as well as of the fine art of dress. In some cities *Independent Clubs* are formed, where the young girls send in the various dishes for the supper, and prepare them, themselves. For instance, if the "*Club*" meets at Mrs. A.'s, she will only need to spread her table with snowy damask, and glittering silver and glass, and her prettiest china dishes, for the contents of the dishes will be sent in by the different members of the "*Club*." Girls need not be forced to learn to cook, sweep and dust, etc., but they should be taught to feel that unless they become adepts in such labors they cannot be worthy of the name of housekeeper, nor a fit wife for any man.

If our girls learn how to make good beds, how to sweep carpets and dust furniture, and make bread and roast meats, and make under-clothing of all kinds, and also to repair and renovate their wardrobes; they will possess a certain kind of self-respect, that no other education can give them; and will also comprehend that without this knowledge they are not worthy of their sex.

A young lady may be able to sing and play, to draw and paint to perfection, but if she is not also instructed in the fine arts of home-life, she cannot lay claim to a superior education, but will be made to feel her deficiencies every day she lives. But if she is a proficient in these arts, she will be more valued and respected as daughter, sister and wife.

A girl who is merely an ornament in the family circle, can never be of the same importance, as one who contributes by her labor and thoughtfulness to its welfare.

To know how to keep house in a superior manner, requires more ability than to be able either to paint or play the piano in perfection, for it is not merely a matter of what shall we eat or what shall we drink, but it combines the best capacities of the human mind. For a good housekeeper must not only be diligent in her work, but she must also possess a good memory, be a good arithmetician, be thoughtful and considerate of others, be able to keep her temper, "no matter if china fall," and put away from her heart all selfishness and narrow-mindedness.

There are many wives and mothers who perform tasks, in conducting their homes in a wise and business-like method, not inferior to what their husbands execute in managing their business affairs; and they should receive equal if not greater credit for the talents they display. For the care of a household, with its nursery duties, as well as its kitchen department, involves a greater demand upon one's patience and perseverance, than it is possible for counting-room, or office to demand.

The equality that the champions of WOMEN'S RIGHTS desire is but an empty name, compared with the true equality found in a marriage, where both husband and wife admit and acknowledge the other's qualifications—the equality in which both perform their duties and obligations with a due sense of each other's short-comings and well-doings, and each allows to the other high praise for good conduct; and such a marriage estate is sure to retain the brightness of the honey-moon, as long as moons shall wax and wane for them.

Hints on Shopping.

It is very poor economy to purchase inferior fabrics because they are cheap, when it is very evident that the material is coarse and slazy; and it will not pay to expend either time or money in making it into garments.

Persons with limited means are very apt, however, to purchase such kind of clothing, because the first outlay is less than would be required to procure high priced goods; and if a calico at six or seven cents looks about as well as one for fifteen cents or twenty cents, it is purchased, and if it can be made up at home, by ingenious hands, and the only extra cost will be for linings, buttons and thread, well and good; but if a dress-maker's aid must be enlisted to cut the dress, it is better economy to purchase the best articles, and make one dress do service for two.

Such mistakes will often be seen through the whole wardrobes of some families; and the result is that they never have anything really handsome, and are always buying and making articles of clothing of poor material, thinking that they are practicing real economy, when to tell the truth, none but rich people can possibly afford to buy poor goods.

And this rule applies strictly to all sorts of goods, carpets and house linen; boots and shoes, as well as to one's wardrobe.

We fairly groan over the time and the toil that some women expend in making up cotton of low price into under-clothing. Just as many stitches are needed for each garment, and the poor cotton will wear out twice as quickly as that of premium quality.

Far better to make three shirts of good cloth, than six of a lower grade. The same thing can be said with regard to flannels for under-clothing. And all-wool Shaker flannel will wear out two or three garments of flimsy cotton-and-wool stuff. In children's clothing especially, one should strive to purchase good materials, those that will wash and bear the wear and tear of an active, out-door life. If it is outgrown, and there is a younger child to wear it, just so many stitches are saved.

Under-clothing in a family of children can be made so as to be serviceable for two or three, as well as for one child. When one starts forth upon a shopping excursion, it is a great saving of time to have a list of the articles required written out legible, just the amount of yards needed, exactly the number of buttons and thread, and the like, that are required.

By this means you will be saved from sudden temptation to purchase what you are really not in want of, in lieu of that which is a decided necessity, and you will be taught to regulate your desires to your wants.

Then trade only with merchants whose reliability and integrity have been tested, and you feel that you will not be cheated, for we all know that in trade "honesty is rarely considered the best policy"—but the usual maxim is, get what you can for your merchandise. In the long run it is the best plan to purchase the needed supplies for a family at one or two stores, and the proprietors will be more likely to sell to you at lowest rates, for a regular customer will often receive favors that are not granted to occasional purchasers. And it is poor policy to spend valuable time in going from store to store, hunting up bargains. Besides, you will often be persuaded to purchase goods that are not essential, merely because they are *so cheap.*

How to Cultivate the Habit of Reading.

There are many housekeepers whose time is so constantly occupied that they do not seem able to find an hour for reading in the twenty-four, and because they cannot take up a book and devote so much time to its pages, they will declare that they have no time to improve their minds. Perhaps we can show them that this is a great mistake.

For there are doubtless a great many five and ten and even fifteen minutes, during the day, that could be given to reading a book or a magazine if it were only at hand. It is not the books that are read in a few hours, or at a sitting, that are of the most service to us, but those that we devour in odd moments, a few pages at a time, which are often the most thoroughly digested, and leave their record indelibly in the mind. The men who have taken high rank in the United States are not always those who had the best advantages for study in their youth, but those who were forced to depend upon self-culture, and to snatch a few moments now and then from laborious occupations to enable them to store their minds with the much-desired knowledge. Henry Wilson, Vice-President of the United States in 1872, owed all his culture to the habit of reading at odd moments; and we believe he could not read at all until he was nearly out of his teens.

It is the habit of reading, rather than the time at your command, that helps you to travel on the road to learning; and many of our scientific men, whose researches have made their names famous, have been able to devote only an hour or two each day to their studies.

If you can learn to use the spare moments that will occur in the midst of your housework, and to read a little in book or newspaper, if it is but a page, you will find your brains stimulated by the exercise, and your labors lightened by the fresh ideas you have received. Pages of poetry can be stored away in the brain, while one tends a child, or finishes the weekly ironing.

Place a volume of *Longfellow's, Lowell's, or Whittier's Poems,* upon the table, opened at some verses whose sentiments cheer your soul, and, as the work progresses, let the words sink so deeply into your memory that time can never efface them.

Poems that are learned before one enters the teens, will be as fresh in the memory when one counts three-score years and ten.

Nothing helps along the monotonous tread-mill round of daily life so much as bright thoughts, which will entertain you while your hands are moulding bread, or fashioning garments. A new idea from some book or newspaper is, to the mind, like the oil which makes your sewing-machine revolve with so much greater ease. The ideas that we recall from books that we have read, will also serve as an incentive to nobler action, and will often become some of the most precious gems in the treasury-house of our remembrance.

All knowledge is made up of atoms, which, perhaps, if taken by themselves, might seem insignificant; but, in the aggregate, they will prove the most valuable weapons for the mind, and the most substantial safeguards for the soul. Doctor Johnson said, "Read anything continuously, and you will be learned." The odd moments which you are inclined to spend in idle longings, or belittling gossip, if occupied in reading, would give you treasures that neither "moth nor rust could corrupt, nor thieves break through and steal."

How to Teach Little Children.

"As if mothers needed any instruction upon this point!" perhaps you will exclaim; "for it surely is easy enough for any one to teach little children."

Pardon us, but we must differ with you, and declare that only those who possess an unlimited and inexhaustible stock of that grand virtue, PATIENCE, are really able to properly instruct little children.

How often we hear a child called dull and apathetic, when the trouble is that the teacher is in fault, and not the child, because she fails to arouse his intelligence and excite his interest! Little children can not be taught to read and spell, to learn short lessons in geography and arithmetic, unless you can animate their minds, and enchain their interest, and this is a task that makes great demands upon the patience of the teacher. Yet it really is of great importance to the child that these stepping-stones in education should be well laid, for they are the groundwork of the knowledge he should acquire, year by year, while he lives. Incorrect spelling; wrong emphasis in reading; indistinct pronunciation; insufficient knowledge of the multiplication table; and a vague idea of the elements of geography, are educational defects often met with in both men and women, and are sure signs of the incapacity of their first teachers.

Little children are happier if they are taught some of the elements of knowledge when about four or five years old. The strongest advocates of the plan of not teaching them anything, until they are six or seven years old, soon learn that it is a great trial to a child to break away from habits of constant play, and that it is far better to give them a slate and pencil, and encourage them to imitate large letters, and to learn to write or print, at the same time that they learn to read. Then teach them to make figures, as well as letters; and then write off the multiplication tables, by turns, until they are completely mastered, and can not possibly be forgotten, while the mind lasts.

But lesson time should be of very short duration; for it is a cruelty to keep an active child confined to either slate or book, after his interest in them has flagged. Five or ten minutes, at first, is quite long enough to keep his attention upon letters or figures. When the letters are mastered, and words can be read, as well as multiplication taught, half an hour will be of greater benefit to the child, if his interest is enchained, than an hour of inattention and frequent reproof.

If you desire to have your children make progress in learning, you must strive to enlist their attention, and make them feel an interest in learning. Of course, there are those who are much more eager to learn than others, but it is possible to make all children take an interest in lessons, if you will only make them see that you are also interested in them; that you consider it the height of happiness to be able to read, and write, and study; and, also, to give them high praise for what they do accomplish. And lead them to talk about their lessons; and, as you read the newspapers, let the little one show you the letters he knows, and do not repel his advances in knowledge, even if you are more deeply interested in the news of the day, than in a–b–c–d's. It is a grave mistake, also, to repel questions, and a still greater one to laugh at the ignorant, or funny sayings of the children; for these little folks are often very sensitive to ridicule, and they will soon cease to seek for information, if their questions are styled foolish or ridiculous.

We well remember how we shrank from ridicule in early life, and how keenly we suffered from ill-advised laughter. It is a great temptation to fond parents to exhibit the intellectual abilities of a clever, bright child; but it is doing him a decided injury to do so; an injury that may be irreparable, both mentally and physically.

The child, doubtless, enjoys being considered a prodigy, and pursues its studies with renewed vigor and delight, until its active brain becomes, as it were, clogged, and loses its power, and the child is not able to concentrate its thoughts and master its lessons. Oftentimes, it comes on so gradually that it is hardly to be perceived, until too late to prevent injury; but parents and teachers should be very careful not to overstimulate a bright child, and, as soon as it shows any signs of languor, the lessons should cease at once; if not entirely, yet in a great degree, and the child be coaxed to active play, and given various amusements that will exercise the body, and restore strength to the brain.

The Best Way to Teach Boys and Girls.

It was once said by the French philosopher, Diderot, that "the best way to educate a child is to tell it stories, and let it tell stories to you."

There is a great deal of philosophy in this remark, and it can be farther extended, for there is an ambulating out-door education as well as a school-room education; the one is obtained by walking among and talking about whatever comes in your way; the other by the study of books, and the use of slates and pencils and blackboards.

It would seem, however, that in many school districts the out-door instruction is altogether too much neglected; education being conducted too much upon the principle of looking out of the window at things instead of visiting them, and learning their properties and uses.

The student can look out of his window and call his horse by five or six different names in as many languages, yet the stable-boy, who can only call it a horse, knows far more about its nature, disposition and properties than the student.

Education consists too much in naming things, when it should be more conversant with their properties and uses. It should connect words with ideas, and as much as they will permit, with objects. If we instruct our children orally, while walking in the streets or fields or forests, upon nature and its treasures, words, ideas and objects will be in closer connection with each other than it would be possible to bring them in a school-room lesson.

And we think that the teacher should take his scholars not only into the fields, but into the streets, and on the railways, and in the shipping yards, and into manufactories; and not only instruct them in all their belongings, but also elicit from them their own impressions, inquiries and thoughts. He should walk and talk with them as well as listen to the lessons that are learned by heart, only to be soon forgotten. The Kindergartens of childhood should be introduced with a wider range for the culture of youth.

How to Economize Time.

A great deal of time and annoyance might be saved if housekeepers would bring some *system* into their daily occupation; and it is an excellent plan to time yourself in the performance of certain duties, and this is particularly so in the preparing of the three meals of the day.

We all know housewives who can so arrange their work that they have plenty of time not only to sew, but to visit and entertain company, and also to read the current literature of the day; while others will work all the time and not accomplish half as much. The secret is in their executive ability; they have a system. They know how to perform their labors in a given time, and set their minds to do it and do not allow themselves to stop and talk, or dilly dally about little things, but take heed to the minutes.

Preparation for dinner can be made to occupy nearly all the time from breakfast until noon, and in many families it does so.

To be sure, there are some dishes, soup for instance, that requires to be cooked all the forenoon, but it needs little care, as it can simmer upon the back part of the stove, and after the potatoes and other vegetables are pared, they can be left to soak in water until time to be placed on the stove. The meat also can be skewered and put into the dripping-pan, until time to be roasted.

Knowledge of the time needed for cooking each article is indispensable to a good cook, and to secure punctuality at meal-time. And no care can preserve an article of food in a tempting condition, if it is intended to be eaten at once, but is kept in the oven sometime before it is served.

It is really a work of art to cook a tempting meal and serve it in a perfect condition; and it takes a good amount of brains to enable one to do it without becoming flurried.

The ability to prepare meals in a short time, however, is an accomplishment that any housekeeper of average capacity can acquire, in a greater or less degree, by thought and practice. Accustom yourself to prepare each article in a given time, looking at the clock, rather than out of the window, when the work is being done. Every one knows how rapidly a meal can be arranged, when an emergency occurs. Why not feel the pressure of an emergency every day, and thus procure time for occupation in some other branches than cookery?

Spread the table between boiling the potatoes and broiling the steak, or basting the meat, and learn to do it expeditiously—having the cloth nicely folded, and all ready to spread in a moment; and be sure that the plates are so hot that the gravy will not congeal into fat, and that the salt-cellars are freshly filled, which should be done directly after breakfast. As we said, at the commencement, system is needed in all things, and nowhere will it work to better advantage than in culinary operations. The merchant and manufacturer might as well expect to manage their business affairs successfully without its aid, as the housekeeper, and the mother of a family, to perform the functions of her office.

To Whiten the Skin.

Lemon-juice and glycerine will whiten the hands and face, beautifully. At night pour a little glycerine into the palm of your hand, and add a few drops of lemon-juice to it; and rub it all over the face, neck and hands. If you are burned by the sun or wind, do it both night and morning.

Care of Family Stores.

The flour barrel should be kept in a dry store-room, and covered tightly, so as to exclude flies and dust. The flour scoop and the sieve can be kept in it, if they are never dampened at all. In many store-rooms there is a special closet for both the flour and sugar barrel, with an opened door to put them in and out, and a close-fitting lid over them; but it is well to keep them also covered with their own heads, which should be fastened together with a slat, or bit of lathing, when first opened. Unbolted flour should be stored in kegs, or covered tubs, or the small tea-chests that are so much used now. It is better, when purchased in small quantities. Indian meal should be kept in the same manner. If it is stirred up occasionally, it is improved; as it is apt to become musty and sour, a little at a time is preferable.

Buckwheat, rice, hominy and ground rice must be purchased in small quantities, also, and kept tightly covered, as they are liable to be infested with small, black bugs. Tapioca, sago, pearl-barley, farina, corn-starch, isinglass, vermicelli, macaroni, arrowroot and oatmeal, are all desirable articles of food, for breakfast or dinner dishes, and they should be found in every store-room, but should be purchased in small quantities, and kept in small wooden boxes, or covered jars. They will give a pleasing variety of food which is healthful, for both children and adults, and often palatable for invalids. Sugars can be kept in quantities, if you are sure of your servants' honesty. Cut loaf for the table, and granulated for preserves, etc., and pulverized for berries and cake. Wooden buckets, or kegs, will store these well. If you will draw a wide chalk-mark around the top of them, no ant can molest the sugars.

Butter should be kept in the coolest and dryest place your surroundings afford, and where there are no spices, or salt fish of any kind. Sweet, fresh atmosphere is very needful for keeping butter sweet. Stone, earthern, or wood, are the best to store it in.

Lard and drippings should be kept as cool and dry as possible, and stone jars are the best for them.

Tea and coffee and spices should not be kept in the same box, as they flavor each other. Neither should they be stored with buckwheat, hominy, oatmeal, or cracked wheat and rice flour, as they impart a disagreeable taste to them.

Raisins, currants and citrons should be stored in a cool place by themselves, in boxes or jars.

Salt is spoiled if kept in a damp place, as it takes up the moisture that is in the atmosphere. It should be carefully covered in glass jars or wooden boxes, and powdered and dried in the oven before using it on the table.

Vinegar is the best if made from cider. It is well to purchase the cider in a keg or barrel, and store it in the cellar with the bung out. If it does not turn to vinegar rapidly, turn it out into large jars, and cover the mouth of them with muslin, and place them in the sun. If "mother" is needed, dip large pieces of blotting paper into molasses and put them into the jars.

To Know if Wines are Colored.

M. de Cherville gives the following useful hints for deciding whether red wines are artificially colored or not. Pour into a glass a small quantity of the liquid, and dissolve a bit of potash in it. If no sediment forms, and if the wine assumes a greenish hue, it has not been artificially colored; if a violet sediment forms, it has been colored with elder or mulberries; if the sediment is red, it has been colored with beet root or Pernambuco wood; if purplish, with logwood; if yellow, with phytolacca berries; if violet blue, with privet berries; if pale violet, with sunflowers.

Prevention of Dampness in Houses.

Damp walls are often a great trouble in houses that are recently built, and in moist climates precautions should be taken to keep the dampness out of the buildings. It can be prevented by a thorough application of asphaltum to the upper portions of the foundation, or to several of the lower tiers of brick, for if the brick work is well covered with it, moisture cannot enter the house. The asphaltum can be dissolved in turpentine.

Another method is also recommended: Take three-quarters of a pound of mottled soap, and shave it up thin into a gallon of boiling water, and spread the hot solution over the outer surface of the brick-work with a large brush, taking care not to work it to a lather.

Let it dry in for twenty-four hours, then wash it over with a solution formed of a quarter of a pound of alum dissolved in two gallons of water, and applied like the soap and water. The work should not be done in damp weather. The soap and alum naturally decompose each other, and form an insoluble varnish which the rain cannot penetrate, and the cause of dampness is effectually removed.

Alum will also prevent mildew. Cloths dipped into strong alum water are proof against this disagreeable fungus.

If alum is put into paste that is used for scrap-books, it will prevent mildew and mold, and it will keep the paste in a good condition for weeks, even if it is left in an open bowl.

As damp walls are sure generators of consumption and rheumatism, it is well to exercise needful precautions to prevent them, and these simple remedies have been recommended by the *Journal of Chemistry.*

How to Brush Clothes.

All woolen clothing is liable to gather dust, and requires an occasional beating to cleanse it, before brushing. The best way to do this is to spread the garment upon a small clothes-horse, and beat it gently with a switch, or a lady's riding-whip, and do not strike too hard, but beat it gently. Rub softly between the hands any spots of mud that seem firmly set, and be sure that the garment is perfectly dry before you commence to clean it.

Two clothes-brushes should be at hand, but do not use the hard one, excepting to brush away fixed dirt. The soft brush will not wear the nap of broadcloth, and it will remove all lint, dust and hairs; an old brush is also better than a new one, for, after the sharp edges of the bristles are somewhat worn, they will take off the dust more effectually. What is called a blacking brush, is one of the best brushes that can be found to clean clothes, but, of course, it must never have been used on boots or shoes.

After dusting a coat, spread it out on a table, with the collar toward your left hand, and brush the inside of the collar, and then the back and sleeves. The nap of the cloth is towards the skirts of a coat, so always brush it downwards. Wipe the dust from the table before you turn the garment on the other side; brush the two lappels, and, lastly, the outside of the collar, and then fold it over and brush in the same way.

A gentleman's wardrobe should be covered with a sheet, if it is not dust proof, and, as clothes are apt to acquire an unpleasant odor, when kept closely shut up for any length of time, they should be aired, at least, once a week.

Be particular to keep the clothes-brushes shut up in a drawer, when not in use, and occasionally wash them in a little saleratus and water, and rub them thoroughly on paper placed over the edge of a table.

How to Put Down Canton Matting.

As there is a right and wrong way of doing everything, it may not come amiss to our readers to learn the right way of putting down Canton mattings, particularly as nearly every one pursues the wrong way.

Most persons cut the lengths to match the floor, and then place them upon it, and drive quantities of tacks up and down the edges. To be sure, this will hold the breadths in place, but it ruins the matting, as every tack will break one or more straws, and it also injures the floor.

Canton mattings are woven on boats, in short pieces, which are afterwards joined together, and, after the matting has been cut in proper lengths, these places should be sewed across with strong carpet thread, to keep them from opening.

Next, sew the breadths together, as you do woolen carpets, and then lay it down on the floor, and tread it into place, and nail by binding over the edges with a doubled piece of buff cambric, and inserting the nails through the bindings.

Mattings put down in this way will last nearly twice as long as when tacked by the breadths. Some very pretty new styles of mattings are now brought from China, and there are no cleaner and cooler coverings for the floor during the Summer's heat, while the woolen carpets can be laid over them in Winter.

How to Make Rag Carpets.

If you desire a firm and durable carpet for your kitchen floor, which can be easily shaken, and turned, and cleansed, make a rag carpet, or else buy one of the carpet dealers, who often keep them on hand.

Old flannels, sheets, under-garments, dresses, in short, anything that can be cut up into long strips, is available in a rag carpet. Even cotton materials can be used, if they are not worn to rags.

Cut the stuffs into strips about an inch in width, and sew each strip together, then roll them into large balls of about one pound weight. Allow from one and a quarter to one and a half pounds of rags for each square yard of carpeting. Of course, your garments must all be well washed and ironed, before you commence to cut them up, and the smaller strips can be sewed together, in a Mosaic or mixed up style, to form a mixed up stripe in the carpet. If you can obtain a few pounds of remnants from a woolen factory, where red, blue and yellow flannels are made, they will brighten the carpet wonderfully. A stripe of various shades of red and maroon, is very effective.

Too much black is not desirable for a kitchen carpet, as it catches dust so quickly; but a little mixed in with red or blue or yellow, does not come amiss, but adds a grace to the carpet. White woolen rags can be colored red, green, or blue or brown with *"Family Dyes."*

For the warp select either brown or slate color or a light gray. Allow one pound of warp for every three and a quarter yards of carpeting.

It is a good plan to keep the exact weight of your warp and rags, and compare them with the weight of the carpet when it is brought back from the weaving mill.

For a kitchen it is a better plan to fasten small hooks or nails around the edges of the mop-boards, and then sew rings on to the carpet to correspond with them, and hook the carpet on, rather than to nail it down, for it can then be taken up on washing days, if the kitchen must be used for that work, and be well shaken and laid down again with but little labor.

To Repaint Iron Bedsteads.

If the old coat of paint is not scaled off in spots so as to make it look rough, it need not be removed, but should be rubbed with glass-paper to make it very smooth. If it is desired to be painted black, take vegetable black, ground in turpentine, with a spot or two of gold size added to fix it, which is flatting.

Give two coats, then varnish with carriage varnish. Use the same method if chocolate is preferred. To make the chocolate hue, take a little purple brown, a pinch of vermilion, ultramarine blue, and a little of the vegetable black. Paint with a small brush.

Care of Brooms and Sweeping.

If brooms are dipped into boiling suds once a week they will become very tough, and will last much longer, and sweep as well as a new broom, after each dipping.

A handful or two of salt sprinkled upon a carpet will carry the dust along with it, and make the carpet look bright and clean.

A very dusty carpet can be cleaned by setting a pail of cold water by the door, and dipping the broom lightly into it, shaking off all the drops, and then sweeping a few yards with it. Repeat the process until the carpet is all swept, and you will be surprised to see how soiled the water becomes. Indeed, if the room is of any size you will need to throw it away and fill it up with fresh water before you finish cleaning the carpet. Snow sprinkled on a carpet, and swept off before it has time to melt, is also an excellent way to clean a much soiled carpet. Indian meal, slightly dampened, can also be used with good effect.

Hints Upon Serviceable Colors in Furniture and Carpets.

It is not always the prettiest hues that will prove the most serviceable, and when one furnishes a house it is well to take some forethought upon the subject and select the colors that not only harmonize well with the walls, etc., but will also wear well. Blue is a favorite hue, yet it is not advisable for rooms that are in constant use, or where the sunshine is constantly admitted, for it fades and soils easily. A bright crimson, although it lights up well, and is a cheery color, is not good to wear, for it fades in spite of the best of care. Green, which was once so much the rage, soon turns dingy and gray, and is if anything worse than crimson. Maroon is an excellent color usually in furniture, and both crimson and maroon wear remarkably well in carpets. But a dark red and black, or green and black carpet is an abomination to its owner, as it shows every speck of dust, and every thread, and a hand broom and dust-pan is in hourly requisition. Various shades of red in carpets are always desirable. In carpets, colors will often wear well that are not economical for furniture coverings. For instance, shaded green carpets with pleasing tints of olive and sage green will wear admirably. But with gray and brown the case alters, for in carpets they are often detestable, but chairs and sofas upholstered in these soft, warm tints, usually prove satisfactory. If more color is required, relieve their somberness with puffs of blue, crimson or green, and your room will present a pleasing appearance.

Directions for Care of House Linen.

When linen has been well dried and aired, and laid by for use, nothing more is necessary but to keep it free from dampness and insects.

Perfumed linen, however, is agreeable to all, and a mixture of aromatic shavings, leaves and flowers can be sewed up in bags and laid in the drawers or on the shelves where it is stored. The ingredients may consist of cedar shavings, powdered sassafras, cassia buds, branches of lavender, rose leaves, stalks of geraniums and sweet verbena. And a few drops of otto of rose, or oil of neroli, can be dropped upon them.

In all cases it will be the best economy to repair both linen and cotton articles before they are sent to the wash. It is also desirable to have each article numbered as well as marked, and to so arrange them that they will be used in regular turn, and all of one set receive an equal amount of wear.

To Wash Cretonne and Chintz so it will Preserve its Colors and Gloss.

When *cretonne* or chintz curtains and furniture coverings have become soiled, take them down carefully, and shake out all the dust that is on the surface, and brush them well. Then boil two pounds of rice in three gallons of water until it is very soft; and pour the whole into a tub. Let it stand until comfortably warm to the hands, and put in the curtains and coverings, and use the rice for soap, washing them thoroughly in it, until they look bright and clean. Rinse in water in which some more rice has been boiled, and strained off from it. This will answer instead of starch. Hang out on the lines until nearly dry, and when it is ironed it will have all the gloss and beauty of new chintz.

If rice is not as readily obtained as wheat bran, substitute the latter, but you will have to use more of it, and it will need more rinsing to free it from the bran than from the rice.

Tea-spoonfuls and Table-spoonfuls.

It has been often discussed by volunteer guardians of the English language, whether one should say spoonfuls, or spoonsful; but it is generally granted that the latter is the most proper form. Yet the matter is of little consequence compared to the time-honored practice of prescribing medicine by the spoonsful.

Every one knows that the table and tea-spoons of the present day vary in their size greatly, and that they have nearly double the fixed capacity of those that were used by our grandparents. When medicine is ordered by a physician, the exact quantity should be given in drops rather than spoonsful, and then there would be no danger of over-dosing those who need the assistance of drugs.

Graduated glasses have been manufactured for more than fifty years, which show exactly how much is held in a spoonful as given in physicians' prescriptions. They are also graduated for drops, and are exceedingly useful in administering all kinds of fluid medicines; and it is surprising that they are so little known.

The Torments of Toothache.

No one, not even a philosopher, can endure the toothache with perfect fortitude and patience, and it is one of the most painful subjects of the moans and groans of humanity. We know that the poet, who wished the most intense torture to the enemies of his country, could think of nothing worse for them than " a twelve month's toothache."

To alleviate and cure this intolerable anguish ought to be the object of every physician. Amongst some new inventions we find a dental syringe, which professes to have great success in curing it. It is a simple apparatus, filled with a fluid preparation, and one end of it is inserted in the cavity, and the other, an elastic bulb, is pressed so that only one or two drops fall upon the nerve. This preparation is harmless to sound teeth, which it is desirable to know, as many of the violent, burning nostrums sold as panaceas to toothache, do much mischief to the teeth that are whole.

Hints on Varnishing.

It is a great benefit to the housekeeper to know how to use varnish, and, with its aid, renew the tarnished furniture of parlor, bed-room, or dining-room.

The first process in the work is to remove all soiled marks, such as smoke, or grease spots, for varnish will not dry well on a soiled surface; therefore, the articles should be washed thoroughly, in soap and water, and wiped dry with a soft flannel. The varnish can be procured at any paint shop, and a small, soft brush is also needed. If articles are varnished in a stove-heated room, and left to dry quickly, they will take a brighter polish, and the appearance of the work will be improved. When you desire to varnish drawings or engravings, first paint them over, with a clear solution of parchment, or what is called sizing. Let it dry in, and then varnish them, dipping the brush in lightly, and taking care not to put on too much varnish at once.

Varnishes are made in three different ways, viz: with alcohol, essential oil, and fixed oil. Alcohol varnishes are made by dissolving resins or gums, in either naphtha or spirits of wine. The resins are broken up into small bits, and placed in a tin pail, or a stone jar, and the spirits or naphtha poured over them. The pail or jar is then placed in a warm situation, and kept there until the gums are wholly dissolved. Such varnishes are as easily applied, as prepared, and their odor is not as disagreeable as that of varnishes made from oil and turpentine. But they are not able to resist moisture, and are not adapted to out-of-door work, as they are liable to crack and peel off, as the naphtha and spirits evaporate and leave a gummy coating that will flake off occasionally. But when oils are used, they will form a solid coating that no moisture can remove, and, therefore, they are much more durable.

When essential oil, or oil of turpentine is used, the older the varnish, the better it will be; and it is best to procure that which has not been recently prepared.

Common resin, dissolved in boiled linseed oil, will make a brilliant varnish, but it is more apt to peel off and crack, than gum-shellac, which is more frequently used for nice work. Gum copal is also used in manufacturing nice varnishes, also mastic, and sandarac and elemi resin.

Varnish for maps is made with six parts of mastic and three of sandarac, rubbed up with powdered glass; the resins and powdered glass are then dissolved, at a moderate heat, in thirty-two parts of spirit; and three parts of Venice turpentine are then added; and the whole is kept at a moderate degree of heat, until well mixed together.

A good copal varnish, for leather-work and similar uses, can be made by dissolving eight parts of powdered gum-copal, in forty-five parts of oil of spike, to which one part of camphor has been added. Heat the oil, and add the powdered gum slowly, stirring it continually.

A moderate degree of heat should be employed in making varnishes, for, if the oil is unduly heated, it may take fire; and varnishes prepared at a low temperature are, also, much more durable.

French Polish.

French polish is a kind of varnish that is much in use, at present, for finishing all kinds of cheap furniture. It is made by dissolving five ounces and a half of gum shellac in one pint of first-proof alcohol. Naphtha is also employed as a solvent, and a little oil is added to increase its brilliancy. Six ounces of gum shellac and one pint of naphtha, and a quarter of a pint of linseed oil, well boiled, will make an excellent polish.

Sometimes a little gum copal, and gum sandarac are added, and the composition is made with a quarter of a pound of gum shellac, and two ounces of gum sandarac, dissolved in one pint of spirits of wine; two fluid ounces of copal varnish, and four ounces of linseed oil are then slowly stirred into it. If the polish is desired to be light-colored, add from two to four drachms of oxalic acid to each pint of the varnish.

How to Use the French Polish.

Before using the French polish the wood should be rubbed as smooth as glass with sand-paper, then pour some of the polish in the center of the surface, and spread it over with a rubber, which should be made of a long strip of thick, woolen cloth, rolled up to a width of from one to three inches, according to the extent of the surface to be polished. Moisten one of the tightly rolled ends with the polish by putting it on to the mouth of the bottle, and shaking it upon it. Then enclose the rubber with two thicknesses of soft linen, fastening the edges of it at the top of the rubber. Moisten the bottom with a drop or two of linseed oil, and apply it with a little of the polish, in one direction only. When one coat has been carefully laid on and dried in, apply another coat, and so on until three have been rubbed in. Then finish the work by rubbing it gently with a piece of linen just moistened with both spirits and oil. French polish can be colored red with alkaret or red sanders wood; or yellow by the use of gamboge or tumeric. Dissolve them in spirits of wine, and strain through a cloth into the varnish.

To Ventilate Closets and Pantries.

Architects sometimes have much to answer for in the way that they plan houses for us to live in; and this matter of ventilation for closets and pantries is rarely considered by them. Yet it is a serious omission, and doubly objectionable in connection with places devoted to the keeping of food or to the storing of linen and clothing, as every good housekeeper fully understands.

Yet, with a little trouble, the evil may be greatly remedied. Call in a house carpenter and ask him to bore a few holes in the upper part of the door, and if it is possible, make an aperture in the walls also, so as to have a good draught through the closet. This is particularly desirable in closets where food is to be kept, for if there is no ventilation the mingled odors of it will soon become stale and offensive.

When closets are apt to become damp and moldy in a hot, rainy season, it is an excellent plan to keep a bucket of fresh lime in the room, as it will absorb the moisture and render the air pure. Of course it will be needful as it becomes fully slaked and dry to renew it in a fresh state, and the slaked lime can be used to purify drains and the like.

This is also an excellent antidote in closets where boots and clothing are apt to become covered with mold. Of course you must not let any water touch the lime, as it might set a wooden bucket on fire, but air slaked lime is harmless.

Bottled Light.

Countless accidents, as every one knows, arise from the use of matches. To obtain light without using them, and so without the danger of setting things on fire, an ingenious contrivance is now used by all the watchmen of Paris in magazines where explosive or inflammable materials are kept. Take an oblong phial of the whitest and the clearest glass, and put a piece of phosphorus, about the size of a pea, into it. Pour some olive oil, heated to the boiling point, into the phial, filling it about two-thirds full, and then cork it tightly.

When the light grows dim its power can be increased by taking out the cork and letting in a supply of fresh air. In Winter it is sometimes needful to heat the phial between the hands to make the oil fluid. Such a light will last for six months at least.

Decoration in Indelible Ink.

Drawings on prints can be imitated with good effect in marking indelible inks upon napkins, tidies and doilies.

A moderately soft quill pen is better adapted to the work than steel pens, and the strokes should be made as rapidly as is possible, with firmness and accuracy. No preparation of the fabric is needed; but the work should be smoothed with a moderately heated iron, before it becomes perfectly dry.

Monograms, initials, etc., can all be finely executed by this method, and there is no prettier way of marking house and table linen.

To Make Walking Sticks.

Tourists often like to carry away a walking stick from some renowned locality as a memento of the place, and simple directions for making them may prove of use to some of our readers.

A handle to a straight stick can be turned by boiling that portion of it from ten minutes to quarter of an hour, in a large pot of water; then bending it round a circular bit of wood, to give it the required curve, and tying it firmly. Let it remain so for several weeks, or until the wood has become perfectly dry, and the support can be cut away. The bending should be done very slowly, so as not to break the fibers of the wood upon which the strain is the greatest, nor to injure the bark. Small oak saplings, when used for sticks, should have the bark removed, and if cut in May they can easily be peeled. Cherry, hazel, holly and white thorn should have the bark preserved, and the knots cut off, not too closely, but so as to present a jagged appearance. Walking sticks hooked at the handle are the best to walk with; and if a coat of varnish is given to them, their appearance is as much improved, as their durability is increased.

To Keep the Hands White and Soft.

Wash them with sand soap, and, immediately afterwards, with fresh water. Then, while they are wet, put into the palm of each hand a very small portion of rose cream, or almond cream, such as gentlemen use for shaving. It can be purchased at any perfumer's. Rub the cream thoroughly into the hands, until it forms a strong lather, which will make them very soft and smooth, as the pores were well opened by the friction of the sand soap.

In some very fine and delicate skins, the sand soap may leave an uncomfortable irritation, and, if it is not immediately removed by the rose cream, substitute oatmeal or Indian meal for the soap, and use the shaving-cream in the same way.

The Need of Cleanliness in Everything.

It has been well said that cleanliness not only has a powerful influence on the health and preservation of the body, but also upon the civilization of the mind. For the least civilized nations are always the filthiest, in their homes. And no one can deny that cleanliness in our garments, as well as in our dwellings, prevents the pernicious effects of dampness, of bad odors, and of contagious vapors arising from substances left to decay. Cleanliness, also, keeps up a healthy circulation, and refreshes and invigorates the blood, and animates and stimulates the mind.

And, as a general thing, we see that those who attend to the cleanliness of their persons and their habitations, are more healthy, and less exposed to diseases, than those who live in a filthy condition, and are only a little higher than the brutes. Cleanliness, also, brings in its train habits of order and arrangement, which are among the first and best methods and elements of happiness in domestic life.

How to Utilize Old Tin Cans.

Canned vegetables and fruits are so generally in use at present, and the empty cans accumulate so rapidly, that our readers may like to learn to what uses they can be put to, for, with but little labor, they really can be made of some service.

To commence, you must take off the tops of them, by placing the cans top side down upon the stove, and letting the solder melt off, and then the lid can be easily removed. Punch holes on opposite sides, near the edges, and you will have a nice little paste or paint bucket, or pail to hang up, to hold matches, or nails, or the like.

Take off the top, cut to a proper shape with a tinman's scissors, and fasten on a handle, by means of a screw through a hole in the bottom, and you have a sugar or a flour scoop. Or, you can make a small saucepan, by cutting down a can to the right size, and leaving a strip on each side, to be bent at right angles; or, better yet, leave it wide enough to wind around a light withe.

A coarse grater, for horse-radish, bread, etc., can be made by cutting a can open, and tacking a piece of it to a flat board, and making the holes with a triangular punch that can be improvised from a nail, or a three-cornered file.

A hanging flower-pot can be made, by boring three or four holes in the edges, and suspending it with cords, and covering the tin with a thick crochet-work in scarlet wools, and adding tassels to it. Fill up the pot with rich earth, and plant the Wandering Jew in it, and it will be "*a thing of beauty*" made from the most useless of rubbish, by the aid of a little ingenuity and a trailing plant.

An Extemporaneous Ice-House.

There are many families who are prevented from storing ice, on account of the cost of an ice-house, although one can be made of the rudest material, and any man, who can handle nails and hammer, can construct it.

Build a pen, in the coldest location about the house—the place where the snow lies the longest in the Spring will be the best. The larger the pen, the better the ice will keep. Make the bottom level, and lay boards along it, not very close together, so that the ice can have a little drainage. Cover the boards a foot in depth with spent tan bark, or sawdust. Nail two boards upon each of the four sides, which should be made of posts, two of them a foot or two higher than the others, and put inner boards, filling up the spaces with the spent tan, or sawdust, or charcoal dust.

Cut the cakes of ice in good shape to handle, and pack them closely, filling up the interstices with pounded ice, and turn a pailful of water over each layer, if it is freezing weather when the ice is packed.

As the pile of ice is built up, nail on some more boards; and when it is piled up about eight feet high, cover the top with, at least, a foot and a half of either tan, sawdust, or straw. If the latter, tread it down firmly.

Make a roof of boards or slabs, slanting to the north, steep enough to shed water, and fasten it on with slabs of wood laid the other way.

Such a pile of ice can be cut, drawn and packed, in a day, by two men, and a yoke of oxen attached to a sled; and it will add greatly to the comfort and health of the family. When it is wanted, lift the ice out at one end, and cover it tightly. An ice-box can be made to hold a large cake of ice, and leave room to keep meat, milk, etc., and it would, doubtless, last from five to six days, so that the pile need not be disturbed daily. The saving in articles of food alone, will more than pay for the cost and trouble in procuring the ice.

The Value of a Scrap-Book.

Every one who takes a newspaper containing various items connected with housekeeping, the toilette, etc., will often regret to have it torn up, on account of some little scrap in it which was of importance to them; but, if a scrap-book was only at hand, the scissors could have quickly transferred the item to its pages.

If you have never been accustomed to preserve short articles, and tiny scraps in this manner, you cannot understand the pleasure you would take in turning over the pages of the book, and reading a bit here and a scrap there. Perhaps a choice bit of poetry will meet your eye, and bring tears to its lids; or a witty anecdote will make the room ring with your laughter. Or, valuable "Hints" or "Recipes" may claim your attention just at the time you needed the knowledge they contain.

Indeed, you can hardly read a single paper at the present time, but you will find something in its columns that is worthy of preservation, and which will be of service to you many times during your life.

Or, you may procure a choice thought, which is far more precious than a jewel set in gold; and, if you will hoard these rare gems, year after year, you will garner up a treasure-book that will not only be of service to yourself, but also to your children and grandchildren, in decades of years yet to come.

And, were it not for such books, this collection of "*Household Hints and Recipes*" would never have been offered for your selection.

Open Windows at Night.

"Very much has been written on this subject, and not always wisely, for whoever sleeps uncomfortably cool will surely not increase in health; and to open a window sky-high when the mercury is at zero, unless a large fire is kept up, is surely an absurdity. Science proves that the colder a sleeping-room is, the more unhealthy does it become, because cold condenses the carbonic acid formed by the breathing of the sleeper; and it settles near the floor and is re-inhaled, and if in a very condensed form, it may produce death.

"Therefore we should be governed by circumstances in ventilation, and never open the windows so that a draught falls upon the bed, or makes the room too cold for comfort. Inflammation of the lungs has often been caused by sleeping in too cold a room.

"An open door and an open fire-place are quite enough for ordinary purposes in very cold weather.

"In miasmatic localities, and these are along water-courses, beside mill-ponds, marshes, bayous, river bottoms, flat lands and the like, it is most important from the first of August until several severe frosts have occurred, to sleep with windows closed, because the cool night air causes the poisonous emanations to become condensed, and make the air heavy; and if they are allowed to enter the sleeping-room, they will corrupt and poison the blood. By daylight these condensations are made so compact by the coolness of the night, that they lie too near the ground to be breathed into the system; but as the sun begins to ascend these miasmas also begin to rise to the height of several feet above the ground, and are then taken freely into the system.

"Therefore the hours of sunrise and sunset are the most unhealthy of all the twenty-four in the localities named, and noon-tide, when the sun is the hottest, is the most healthful portion of the day, because the miasm is so much rarified that it ascends rapidly in the air.

"The general lessons to be learned," says Dr. Hall, "are:—1st. Avoid exposure to the outdoor air in miasmatic localities, for the hours including sunrise and sunset. 2d. Have a blazing fire on the hearth of the sitting room to rarify the air. 3d. Take breakfast before going out of doors in the morning, and tea before sundown, and do not be out late at night."

The Use of Paper in the Household.

Newspapers and wrapping papers can be put to many valuable uses in the household. Few housekeepers can find the time to black their cooking stoves every day; but even if they wash them daily, in clean water, they will soon become quite shabby; but if they are rubbed over with newspaper, every morning, after the dishes are washed, they will keep black for a long time. If a spot of grease or stain of some kind adheres, moisten the paper a little and rub it off.

Newspaper or wrapping paper will keep the outside of the tea and coffee-pot, and all tin utensils about the stove brighter than the old way of washing them often in soap-suds.

Rubbing with dry paper is the best way to polish knives, spoons and brasses, after they have been scoured clean, and if a little wheat flour is sprinkled over the paper while rubbing them, it will make them shine like silver or gold. For polishing lamp chimneys, and for washing mirrors and windows it is far preferable to any kind of cloth.

Preserves and pickles will keep much better if brown paper is tied over them. Canned fruits are also better if a piece of writing paper is laid directly on the top of the fruit.

Paper is much more serviceable to put under carpets than straw or hay. It is also warmer, and does not rattle as you step upon it. There is a kind of paper especially manufactured for this purpose. There are papers also in use for sheathing the walls of the house, and for overlaying the roofs. Indeed the uses for paper have increased greatly in the past quarter of a century, and whoever will invent paper dishes of cheaper manufacture that those of *papier-mache*, will be a benefactor to his race.

Recipe for A Lady's Dress.

The following recipe for a lady's dress, is found in the works of Tertullian:

Let simplicity be your white, and chastity be your vermilion; dress your eyebrows with modesty; and your lips with reservedness. Let instruction be your earrings, and a ruby cross the front pin of your head. Employ your hands in housewifery; and keep your feet within your own doors.

Let your garments be made with the silk of probity, the fine linen of sanctity, and the purple of chastity.

Hints Upon Repairing Overcoats.

Overcoats are more troublesome to repair than any other garment worn by gentlemen. They are usually obtained at ready-made clothing warehouses, and are not always made of durable materials, and sometimes the linings will last longer than the outsides, and perhaps the garment will seem to be too good to throw away, although it is not an easy job to patch it without any pieces like the original stuff at hand; and yet the farmer does not like to give it up, and use his go-to-meeting coat, to do the chores, carry in wood, and go to the mill.

So we will tell his wife how to make it over quite as good as new. Rip off the buttons, and sew up the large rents in the backs or fronts; and rip out the sleeves; and then spread the garment upon the floor, and measure it with a yard measure, to find out how much material is needed to cover it. Then buy some kind of light soft cloth, like tweed or water-proof, or Kentucky Jean, which is a mixture of cotton and wool. Pin the new cloth very smoothly over the back—there need not be any seam in the middle, but allow deep seams for the sides and shoulders. Let it remain pinned on very closely, and proceed in the same way to cut the fronts; baste up the seams under the arms to fit exactly. If you pin the cloth on the wrong side out, you will manage better. Cut the sleeves in the same way. Sew up the seams, press them smoothly; set in the sleeves. Then cut the facings for the fronts, and sew them on, from the point where the collar is to be put on, down the front to the bottom of the coat. Finish the sleeves at the wrist with bindings or facings. Hem the cover to the coat around the bottom. Put the cover thus made on to the coat, basting it closely on to the seams under the arms, and on the shoulders. Cut the upper side of the collar an inch wider than the under side, and when made put it on to the coat collar. The old pockets will answer if they are whole. Cut a place in the new cloth for them, and finish with binding or pocket-lid as preferred. Button-holes can be worked over the old ones. Then sew on the buttons, and the result will be a whole and respectable looking coat. If the coat is faded but not worn out, rip it apart and turn it.

How to make Cloth Water-proof.

Take a good article of Scotch tweed, and dip it into a bucket of soft water that holds about two gallons, in which has been dissolved half a pound of sugar of lead, and the same quantity of powdered alum. To prepare the solution, dissolve the ingredients in some warm water, then pour it into clear water, and stir it up well. Let it stand and settle until it is perfectly clear, and then dip in the cloth, and let it soak for twenty-four hours, and hang it up without ringing it at all. Garments thus treated will entirely exclude all moisture, and are better in every way than the so-called water-proof cloths.

The Clothing We Wear.

Dr. Nichols, of the *Journal of Chemistry*, says: The color of our clothing is by no means a matter of indifference to our comfort. White and light-colored cloths reflect the heat, while black and dark-colored ones absorb it; therefore white should be the fashionable color in Summer, for it reflects heat well and prevents the sun's rays from passing through and heating the body.

But if white is the best color for Summer, it does not follow that black is the best for Winter. It must be remembered that black radiates heat with great rapidity. Give a coat of white paint to a black steam radiator which is capable of rendering a room comfortably warm at all times, and the temperature will fall at once, although the heat-producing agency remains the same as before. A black garment robs the body of a larger amount of heat than white, and consequently the latter color is the best for Winter garments. So we see that it should be worn both Summer and Winter.

Although this statement may seem like blowing hot and cold, it is nevertheless true. Let those who are troubled with cold feet, and who wear dark-colored stockings, change to white, and see if the difficulty is not partly or wholly removed.

How to Wash Fine Under-clothing.

A leading firm of importers of under-clothing, give the following directions for washing merino, silk, and lamb's wool under-clothing. Scrape one pound of bar soap into sufficient water to melt it. Let it come to a boil, and add three table-spoonfuls of aqua ammonia to it, and two of powdered borax. While it cools, beat it thoroughly, and it will look like a jelly. When needed for use, take a tea-cupful of it to four gallons of warm water, not too hot, and rinse the under-clothing in it, drawing them repeatedly through the hand, but do not scrub them much, for that pulls the material, and also wears it out. Rinse them in clean, lukewarm water, ring and stretch them to their proper shape, and dry in the open air if possible.

The material used in manufacturing silk underwear being an animal product, it is absolutely needful that nothing but the best quality of soap should be used, and if too hot water is turned upon it, it will yellow and shrink it; while all kinds of washing compounds, other than the above, will destroy the nature of the material.

To Remove Mold.

There are two excellent recipes for removing spots of mold from fabrics—one is by just rubbing them over with butter, and then applying potash moistened in a little water, and rubbing the spot until all traces of it disappear, and washing it in plenty of water to take out the potash.

By the other method the mark should first be wetted with yellow sulphide of ammonia, by which it will be immediately blackened. After letting it penetrate the material for a minute or two, wash it off and remove the black stain with cold, weak chlorohydric acid; wash off well with warmish water.

Scotch Method of Washing Woolen Shawls.

Scrape one pound of bar soap into sufficient water to melt it, and let it boil. As it cools, beat it with a spoon, and add three table-spoonfuls of spirits of turpentine, and one of spirits of hartshorn. Wash the articles thoroughly in this, allowing three table-spoonfuls of the jelly to each gallon of lukewarm water. Rinse in nearly cold water until all the soap is out. Then rinse in salt and water. Fold between two sheets, and iron over the sheets.

Knitted and crocheted shawls, cleaned in this manner, will look like new. The salt need not be used unless there are delicate colors that may spread in drying.

To Restore Black Silk Dresses.

Rip the dress apart and shake or brush out all the dust. If any grease spots are visible, put a bit of brown paper over them, and place a moderately heated iron upon it, until the grease is absorbed in the paper.

Then spread the silk breadths upon a clean table, and sponge them with a mixture of stale beer or ale, water and ammonia, in the proportion of a tea-cupful of ale or beer to a pint of cold water, and a bit of carbonate of ammonia as large as a walnut. Moisten the sponge but slightly, and rub it over the silk evenly, so as not to streak it, and as each breadth is cleaned, roll it around a newspaper into a round roll. Lay it aside to dry, covering each roll with a cloth to keep off the dust. When nearly dry unroll the silk, and shake it well so there will be no wrinkles in it, and roll it up again and let it lie until dried.

Do not put an iron upon it, as it takes away the fresh appearance of the silk.

To Remove Iron Rust.

Cover the spots with table salt, and squeeze enough lemon juice over it to dissolve the salt, spread the cloth in the sun, and the spots will soon vanish. Then wash it out in hot water.

Starch finely powdered, can be substituted for the salt, and the same process repeated. If the spots are not wholly gone apply another portion.

If a lemon is not obtainable, rub each side of the cloth with yellow soap until it makes a paste; then spread a mixture of starch and water over the soap, and expose to the sun and air. If the stains do not disappear in a few hours, repeat.

The Rag Bag.

"Are you housekeeper enough to keep a rag-bag?" asked a friend of a young bride.

"If I were not, I certainly should not call myself a housekeeper," she replied.

Not keep a rag-bag! Why the very idea implies that one is ignorant of the first principles of economy. What would become of all the little scraps and old rags if we had not such a receptacle for them. We know of ladies who keep themselves well supplied with pans, dippers and skimmers from the profits of the rag-bag; and wise housekeepers often have two bags, one for white rags and another for colored ones, so as to do away with the trouble of separating them when the rag-man calls, because white rags will always command a much higher price than colored or mixed ones. If a rag-bag is made of strong twilled cotton or thick bed-ticking, it will last a generation. The pretty fancy scrap-bags for the sewing room are also necessary objects, as they keep many a thread from the carpet and many a tiny scrap from the fire-place.

How to Pour Out Tea.

At breakfast a grown-up daughter should relieve her mother from the trouble of pouring out tea and coffee, and, by giving her mind to the business, and learning all her mother's ways, she will make it agreeable for her to resign the office.

Some young ladies are very earnest to be of use, and to take some of their mother's duties upon themselves, where the family is a large one, and the duties onerous; but by not entering into the true spirit of the business, and learning to do it in the best way, their services have not been acceptable; but, far from being conscious that the fault was in themselves, they have blamed their mothers for not being allowed to relieve them of some of their burdens.

There is more to be learned about pouring out tea and coffee, than some young ladies are willing to believe. If these beverages are made at the table, which is by far the best method to pursue, they require experience, judgment and exactness; if they are brought on the table already prepared, it will still require judgment so to apportion them, that they shall prove sufficient in quantity for the family party, and that the elder members of the family shall have the strongest cups.

Persons will often pour out tea without being aware that the first cup is the weakest, and that the tea grows stronger as you approach the bottom of the tea-pot, and will, therefore, bestow the poorest cup upon the visitor or the head of the family, and give the strongest to themselves.

Where several cups of equal strength are desired, it is better to pour a little tea into each, and then go back, inverting the order as you fill them up, and the strength will be apportioned properly. This is so well understood in England, that an experienced pourer of tea waits till all the cups of the company are returned to her, before she fills any a second time, that all may share alike.

You should learn every one's taste in the matter of sugar and cream, too, in order to suit them in that respect; but, in many families, the sugar and tea are passed separately, and each person helps himself. Yet tea is better flavored when it is poured upon the cream.

Delicacy and neatness can be shown in the manner of handling and rinsing cups, and in using the cream jug, without letting the cream run down from the lip. There are a thousand little niceties which will occur to you, if you give due attention to the business, and resolve to do it with the thrift of a good housekeeper, and the ease and dignity of a refined lady. When you have once acquired good habits in this department, it will require less attention, and you will always do it in the best way, without thinking much about it.

A very happy match once grew out of the admiration felt by a gentleman on

HOUSEHOLD HINTS AND RECIPES.

seeing a young lady preside well at the tea-table. Her graceful and dextrous movements there, first fixed his attention upon her, and led to a nearer acquaintance.

How to Wash Straw Matting.

Take a pail half-full of hot water, a plate with some dry, unsifted Indian meal and a perfectly clean long-handled mop. The matting should first be swept very clean, so that no dust remains upon it; then scatter the dry meal evenly, all over the floor. Dip the mop into the pail of water, wring it out so dry that it will not drip at all, and rub one breadth at a time, always lengthwise of the straw, and use clean water for each breadth. Rub it hard, and when the mattings dry, the meal can easily be brushed off from it. It should always be done upon a warm, sunny day, when the windows can be left open, and the matting dried quickly.

To Insert Screws into Plastered Walls.

It is often found impossible to fasten brackets, strips of wood, etc., to plastered walls by means of screws, for they cannot be made to hold firmly, as the plaster breaks away with every turn of the screw. The best way to do it is to enlarge the hole to about twice the diameter of the screw, and fill it up with plaster of Paris moistened just enough to be pliable to the fingers, and bed the screw in the soft plaster. When it has hardened, the screw will be held very strongly, and will bear considerable weight upon it.

To Repair Leaky Roofs.

Melt together in an iron pot two parts by weight of common pitch, and one part of gutta-percha. This will form a homogenous fluid that is much more manageable than gutta-percha alone. To repair leaks in roofs, gutters or other surfaces, carefully clean out of the cracks all dirt and rubbish; and slightly warm the edges with a plumber's soldering iron, then pour the cement in a fluid state upon the cracks while hot, finishing up by going over the cement with a moderately hot iron, so as to make a good connection and a smooth joint. This recipe will repair zinc, lead or iron fissures, and is an excellent cement for aquariums.

The Value of Friends.

Our enjoyment in this life is very much influenced by our friendships, and we do not hesitate to assert that no one is happy who does not possess friends. You may become as rich as Commodore Vanderbilt, who was the Crœsus of New York, may carry on extensive operations, and order regiments of employes to do your bidding, yet unless you possess warm-hearted, true friends, you are of all men most miserable. The Almighty designed that friendships should be a great source of pleasure to all, and if you do not fully appreciate that pleasure you do not fulfill the destiny that God intended for you.

"There is nothing," wrote Montaigne, "to which nature seems so much to have inclined us, as to society."

Neander declared "him to be happy that had the good fortune to meet with but the shadow of a friend."

Aristotle said, "Good legislators have more respect to friendship than to justice."

"Without friends," exclaimed Bacon, "the world is but a wilderness." No recipe openeth the heart but a true friend, to whom you may impart griefs, joys, fears, hopes, suspicions, counsels, and whatever comes the nearest to the heart.

No man imparts his joys to his friends without increasing his enjoyment, and no man shares his griefs with his friend, without feeling their burden lessened.

Friendships make a fair day in the affections, even out of storms and tempest; and they make daylight in the understanding, out of darkness and confusion of thought.

Bacon also observes: "The best way to represent to life the manifold uses of friendship, is to cast and see how many things there are which a man cannot do for himself; and then it will appear that it was a sparring speech of the ancients to say, that a *friend is another himself;* or that a friend is far more than himself."

And just as far as you withdraw yourselves from the sympathy and companionship of human beings, just so far are you liable to become selfish, morose, and disagreeable. No one can expect to obtain happiness and contentment by shutting up the heart against outsiders, and becoming wholly absorbed in one's own family, or in business or professional pursuits.

And when sickness, adversity and trials come, then you will learn by experience, that your friends can do kindnesses for you that no money can obtain, for they can speak words of solace to your ears, and give your fainting soul strength to endure unto the end.

Therefore it should be your aim to make for yourselves a band of true and tried friends, not mere acquaintances, who will stand aside when your skies grow black, but fast, staunch friends, who will never leave nor forsake you while life lasts.

In neighborhoods, a feeling of good fellowship should be cultivated with those whose companionships will be agreeable and beneficial, and every opportunity should be improved to establish an intimate friendship with those who will be as firm as the rocks, in your day of trouble.

How to Save Coal in Open Grates.

The most practical suggestion yet made towards economizing the use of coals seems to be in the use of solid bottoms in ordinary fire-grates. It has been asserted, and indeed proved, that in any fire grate, not exceedingly small, a plate of iron placed upon the bars will nearly halve the consumption of coal, and also reduce the smoke, and keep up a cheerful, free-burning fire. Quite sufficient air will enter through the front bars, and all poking should be avoided, and the fire will continue until all the coal is consumed, which will be done without leaving much ash or dust. Any housekeeper can try the experiment. A sheet of iron to fit easily into the grate will cost but a quarter of a dollar, and the coal bin will not need to be replenished so frequently.

The Best Time for Painting Houses.

The best time for painting the exterior of houses is late in the Autumn or during the Winter, when it is sunny and warm. Paint applied at that season, it is said, will last twice as long as when it is done in early Summer or hot weather, because in the former case it dries slowly and becomes hard, like a glazed surface, and is not easily affected by the weather, or worn off by the beating of storms.

But in the Summer, the oil which is mixed with the lead, strikes into the wood at once, and leaves the lead on the surface, so that it will crumble and flake off very quickly.

This last difficulty, however, can be prevented, although at an increased expense, by brushing over the surface with raw oil. But it is always best to paint when the ground is frozen, and no dust flies, and insects are not preserved in the mixture.

How to Fix the Clock.

When the clock stops do not take it to the repair shop, until you have tried your hand at fixing it by the following directions:

Take off the pointers and the face; unhook the pendulum and its wire. Remove the ratchet from the "tick" wheel, and the clock will run down with great velocity. Let it go; the increasing speed will wear away the gum and dust from the pinions, and the clock will clean itself.

If you have any machine oil, put the least bit on the axles. Then replace all the parts of the machine exactly, and nine times out of ten it will run just as well as if it had been taken to the clock-makers, for this is the way most clocks are repaired. If instead of a pendulum the clock has a watch escapement, it can be taken out in a moment without taking the works apart, and the result is the same. It takes about twenty minutes to clean a clock, and you can save a dollar by doing it.

Some Facts Worth Knowing for Housekeepers.

"*Every wise woman buildeth her house,*" said Solomon; but we believe that there are many women, at the present day, who know very little concerning the practical details of house-building, and, if they would pay a little more attention to them, or, at least, to the interior arrangement, there would be many more comfortable and convenient houses. We have never heard of a woman becoming an architect, or an upholsterer, or a painter; yet she might excel in both of these professions, and would comprehend more fully than a man often does, the necessity of doing the work thoroughly, so that neither doors nor furniture would warp, nor paint blister; and the arrangements for the closets and the kitchen would be more complete, while she would also understand what colors are best adapted for nursery and dining-room use.

Women ought to understand these things, and study into them, as they do concerning the most desirable and artistic hues for draperies and paper-hangings; for it is much more desirable that the house should be conveniently arranged, and the paint of durable colors, and well prepared, than that the parlor should be papered in the latest fashion, and the chambers artistically furnished, and the draperies of the windows be made of the rarest laces or chintzes.

When the first rough coat of plaster is laid upon the walls, and the doors and window-casings are placed then the housekeeper should feel that she can give special directions concerning the finishing.

If she desires to finish the house in the most economical manner, she can have the following recipe for sizing applied to the walls: Melt two pounds of common glue, in a little boiling water, and add to it, when thoroughly dissolved, eight gallons of cold water. Then stir into it twelve pounds of whiting.

This will make a smooth finish, which can be washed in cold milk and water, every Spring and Fall. It can be applied with a common whitewash brush, and will form a good basis for papering. It can also be tinted with a little yellow ochre, to form a lemon-colored wash, or Spanish brown, for an ashes-of-roses tint, and a little cobalt will give to it a light gray hue.

But, if there is any dampness upon the walls, neither whiting, nor glue, nor paper-hangings will do, but an oil paint must be applied; and it can be bought in cans, ready-mixed for use. If the housewife desires to try her hand at painting, she must procure a No. 5 brush, and, if she can get one that is partly worn, it will be more serviceable. She will also need a step-ladder, and she can tie a small paint-pot around her waist. When putting aside the paint, pour cold water over it to keep the dust out, and put the brushes into the water. In laying on paint, dip the brush only an inch into the paint, and strike it once or twice against the side of the pot, to shake off all drops. Then make straight strokes of the brush, with the grain, not across it, drawing downward or vertical, and from left to right on horizontal surfaces; and carry the brush off, not lifting it, at the end of each stroke.

Make the first coat the lightest and the thinnest one, stopping all cracks and holes with putty, after the paint is dry. Paint all crevices, bevels and headings before you do the flat surfaces next them, with a full brush. Work the paint well into the wood by passing the brush vigorously back and forth when each coat is on.

For sashes and fine work use a No. 4 brush, and carry it only one way, not back and forth. Protect glass in sashes, and walls at the side of mouldings, by tacking a strip of paste-board, several inches wide, against the surface next the work to catch dashes of paint.

If spots of mildew or blisters appear on wall paper in a room where steam does not penetrate, there is no use in saving the paper, but strip it off, by wetting it with sal-soda dissolved in water, and then it will peal off easily.

Make a paint by mixing with every gallon of boiled linseed oil, one quarter of a pound of glue, which has been dissolved in just enough boiling water to make it liquid, and add any of the colors mentioned above for white-wash to give it tint.

Another more effectual coating is made of five pounds of pure India rubber melted in a gallon of boiled linseed oil. This mixture can be heated in a tin pail placed in an iron kettle of boiling water, so that it will not take fire.

Paint the wall with this, and it can never be penetrated by dampness, while one gallon of the preparation will coat fifty yards of surface.

One gallon of the oil and glue requires twenty pounds of dry paint ground in it, to put two coats upon forty square yards of surface. Use nothing but the boiled linseed oil for the work, as the raw takes a long time to become dry.

A good drying oil can be made by boiling one ounce of sugar of lead and one ounce of sulphate of zinc with two ounces each of litharge, red-lead and umber, in a gallon of linseed oil until it will scorch a feather.

White-lead gives the most body to paint, and will last the longest, but it will turn yellow, and it is often mixed with inferior pigment. Zinc white will keep its whiteness the longest. Three coats will be much more lasting than two on inside work. The first is called the priming, and is the only coat in which oil should be used, for in the upper coats it is apt to turn yellow by exposure to the air. The cheapest priming is given by a coat of oil on which whiting is rubbed, filling all the pores of the wood with a thin putty, which not only preserves it well but gives a fine surface for the paint.

A good common finish can be made by mixing a second coat of zinc white with enough oil to moisten it, and thinning it to the consistency of paint with naphtha; then a third coat of zinc in naphtha, with one-third Damar varnish mixed into it. This mixture will give a pure glossy white, which is the pride of neat housewives, and all fly specks and soil can be wiped off with a cloth dipped into warmish water, and squeezed nearly dry.

The most expensive but also the most durable white finish is made in this way. Put on one coat of shellac varnish, then four successive coats of pure zinc ground in oil, and mixed with turpentine. Each coat must be allowed to become thoroughly dry before another is added, and the whole should be rubbed very smooth with pumice stone. Then apply two coats of French zinc in varnish, and you will have a hard, shining surface, as fine as enamel.

Honor Your Occupation.

It is a good sign when women are proud of their work, and you may be sure that you cannot excel in it, and understand your trade or occupation, if you are inclined to find fault with it, and to consider yourself an object of pity, because you are under the necessity of earning a livelihood. And if you fret about it you will not only destroy all your own comfort, but also that of your employers; and if you change your work you will often find that you have not improved your position. But, on the contrary, if you will put your heart into it, and try to do your daily tasks thoroughly, and in the best possible manner, you will not only be happier, but you will also make others happier.

There is no station in life that has not its own peculiar cares and vexations; and no woman can escape the annoyances of life, no matter what may be your occupation, whether you are wife, mother and housekeeper, or dress-maker, milliner or shop girl, you must endure the inevitable burdens of life.

Life in all its devious windings is full of trials, unwelcome duties, and spirit-wearing necessities; and it is the very wantonness of folly for a woman to fret over its cares and anxieties, for they must be endured; therefore it is far wiser to shoulder them bravely, and not to brood over them, and thereby give them strength to weaken both mind and heart.

A woman has power given to her to make the homeliest toil pleasant and beautiful, if she only has the sense to work with the right spirit. So let us beg of you to honor your occupations, whatever they may be, and to identify them with pleasant associations; for Heaven endowed us with the powers of imagination, not only to make us poets, but to give us the ability to transform ugliness into beauty.

Heart-varnish will beautify innumerable defects, and conceal many deformities of life.

Look on the bright side always, and accept your lot uncomplainingly, and set yourself to work to enrich it and plant it with blossoming vines and plants of kindness and good-will to all. There is something in the most disagreeable occupations of life around which a woman can twine pleasant fancies, from whose out-growth an honest pride can be developed.

Praise the Children.

There is an old superstition that praise is too precious an article to be bestowed upon the children, that it is too rich a diet for their moral and mental digestion.

Indeed, some parents are so afraid that their children will be injured by it, or that they will become too self-satisfied and proud, that they never suffer them to taste a sweet morsel of praise, but in the end, they will often find that such a course is exceedingly disastrous to their well-being; for it may engender a melancholy hopelessness of disposition, a self-distrust that is pernicious to success in life, or else it weans the children from their home, and teaches them to find pleasure in more congenial companionship. We consider that praise is quite as needful for the healthful growth of childhood, as sunshine is for the development of flowers; and there is no child who does not long for it, and require it to bring out the best side of his heart and mind. It is the most desirable and the legitimate reward of well-doing, no matter how trifling may be the affair. If your child picks up your handkerchief, thank him for the act, and thus inspire him with a desire to do little deeds of kindness. Thomas Hughes says that you never can get a man's best out of him without praise.

We know that you never can excite a child to his best behavior if you deny him the sweet breath of commendation; and we fully believe that many a sensitive child dies of hunger from want of it; and many a child, starving for the praise that its mother refuses to bestow upon it, runs eagerly after those whose flattery is so dangerous to its soul.

Motives of common justice alone, should teach mothers to praise their children for good behavior on all occasions, and thus instill into their minds a sense of goodness.

Of course there is a decided difference in the minds of children, and there are those who cannot endure much praise, any more than they can bear a diet of sweets in too large quantities; and wise mothers will soon learn to bestow praise in doses graduated according to the appetites of the children; and to sandwich blame and praise together so judiciously that they well affect the taste as pleasantly as the toothsome sandwich of our tables.

To Cure Children of Biting their Finger-Nails.

Both girls and boys are apt to indulge in the bad habit of biting their finger-nails, as determinedly as though they were rodents, and must gnaw at something continuously.

It is a singularly morbid craving peculiar to some temperaments that cannot remain long at rest; and neither appeals to their pride of appearance, nor to their sense of cleanliness are of any avail with nail-gnawers, therefore the only hope of success in breaking up such a pernicious course that not only destroys the symmetry of the fingers, but also their nice perception of touch, is to compel them to dip the tips of their fingers every night and morning, into a strong solution of aloes, an intensely bitter drug, so offensive to the taste that even in sleep the nails will be withdrawn quickly if placed on the lips, but yet not unhealthy. A decoction of tobacco will also do as well, but sometimes it will produce nausea as well as shuddering disgust. Yet a little of that is better than to go through life with misshapen, distorted fingers, produced by the horrible propensity to bite them. Be firm with the first remedy, however, insisting that the fingers shall be wetted with the aloes, and it shall not be washed off; and you will rarely fail to effect a cure.

The Charm of Reserve.

Do not be too anxious to give yourself away, to wear your heart upon your sleeve. It is not only unwise, but it is wrong to make your secret soul common property. For you bring the delicate things of the heart into contempt by exposing them to those who cannot understand them.

If you throw pearls before swine, they will turn again and rend you. Nor, again, should you claim too much openness as a duty due to you, from your child, your friend, your wife or your husband. Much of the charm of life is ruined by exacting demands of confidence. Respect the natural modesty of the soul; its more delicate flowers of feeling close their petals when they are touched too rudely. Wait with curious love, with eager interest, for the time when, all being harmonious, the revelation will come of its own accord, undemanded.

The expectation has its charm, for as long as life has something to learn, life is interesting; as long as a friend has something to give, friendship is delightful, and those who wish to destroy all mystery in those they love, to have everything revealed, are unconsciously killing their own happiness.

It is much to be with those who have many things to say to us, which we cannot bear now. It is much to live with those who sometimes speak to us in parables, if we love them.

Love needs some indefiniteness in order to keep its charm. Respect, which saves love from the familiarity which degrades it, is kept vivid when we feel that there is a mystery in those we love which comes of depth of character.

Remember, therefore, that in violating your own reserve, or that of another, you destroy that sensitiveness of character which makes so much of the beauty of character; and beauty of character is not so common as not to make it a cruel thing to spoil it.—*Rev. Stafford A. Brooks.*

How to Kill Animals Without Pain.

There are doubtless many persons who possess four-footed friends that have become so old that they cannot enjoy life, and are also an annoyance to the household; and they would gladly put an end to their sufferings, but cannot endure the thoughts of shooting them, yet would gladly adopt some means that would be merciful.

To put horses to death painlessly, take a large sponge—at least seven or eight inches in diameter, and saturate it thoroughly with chloroform, perhaps five or six ounces will be enough; put the sponge into a paper or cloth bag that can be drawn over the horse's nose, but not so tightly as to interfere with its breathing, for that would cause death by suffocation, and not a painless death. But if it is put on rightly, in a few moments the animal becomes unconscious, and in eight or ten minutes is dead. Or if you prefer, you can put eight ounces of chloroform into a glass bottle, and insert the nose of it into the horse's mouth, and turn it down his throat, and in a few moments he falls asleep, never to wake.

For dogs or cats, a similar process can be used, and the sponge can be applied while the animal sleeps, and a handkerchief or bit of cloth thrown over the head, to keep the fumes close to the nose. Or the chloroform can be turned into a little milk, and the animal will lap it up, and soon become unconscious.

We have known several cases where pet dogs, which had become superanuated, were thus put to sleep forever.

The Value of Good Roads in Communities.

It is an old and true, though trite saying that, "*What's everybody's business, is nobody's.*" And it holds good in respect to country roads in almost every locality where the faulty system in vogue at present exists. Show us a locality where the roads are well made and well kept, and we will show you a thriving and intelligent community.

That good roads add very much to the value of the real estate around them, is not only a well-known fact in the experience of any one who has ever been on the search for a farm or dwelling place; but they have been considered as the chief test of the state of civilization in which people and nations have existed. We estimate the intelligence of the Ancient Romans highly, from the fact that they made roads, upwards of two thousands years ago, which serve the purpose of the European nations which use them to-day. These roads were also a great agency in bringing to a state of civilization our ancient ancestors, who at that time dressed principally in blue paint in the Summer, and shivered in Winter with the shelter of a sheepskin around their loins.

It is a matter of surprise, that while nationally, we, too, are improving our public domain, and bringing under civilizing influences our wild races, by assisting in the building of such a system of railroads as has never before been dreamed of, we allow our common country roads to be almost unfit for travel, by neglect or badly applied efforts.

If we were to apply the test of roads (to say nothing of school-houses) to many districts that we know, we should infer that they were decidedly behind in the "march of improvement," and had a pretty long road to travel, before they got abreast of the present order of things.

How to Make a Model Village.

In these days,

"*When art and labor meet in truce,*
And beauty 's made the bride of use,"

it behooves those of us who live in villages to exert ourselves to make them models of neatness and elegance; and to plant trees by the road-sides, and flowering plants and vines about our houses; and strive to make our surroundings as attractive as possible, not only to the inmates of the house, but also to the passer-by.

Model villages ought to form the rule rather than the exception; and in the green-leaved Summer-time there are thousands of them scattered through the United States, under the rocky brows of its high hills, or beside the peaceful running streams, that turn the mill below the dam, whose loveliness attracts the admiration of all who behold it.

Every house seems shaded by green trees, and looks like the home of peace; while trailing plants adorn its piazzas, and hang about its windows, and brilliant flowers, of every hue, lift up their fragrant chalices to the sunlight in the garden. But wait until Winter comes, and then behold the metamorphose! In many cases the roads are deeply cut up by heavy teams, and are ankle deep in mud; while the houses are no longer concealed by the graceful draperies of green, and show themselves in their true colors, with worn-off paint, and dilapidated fences; and perhaps the broken windows of the homes of the poorer classes, are ornamented with rimless hats, or stuffed with rags to keep out the chill blast.

A VILLAGE IMPROVEMENT SOCIETY would soon change all this; and its influence would be of the greatest importance in promoting good order and cleanliness, as well as beauty and elegance. A strawberry party, or a fair could be held to procure the needful funds to obtain and plant trees, and to arrange sidewalks; and if its members began by only making their own homes and grounds neat and attractive, the good work would have been commenced, and others would soon follow their example; and when the Autumn winds laid the green leaves low, all the beauty of the place would not be destroyed. In St. Johnsbury, Vt., one can see a model village, where the munificence of the manufacturers of Fairbanks' scales have given an impetus to both art and labor, and each householder strives with the other to maintain good order.

How to Train a Servant.

In all attempts to train persons in a very low stage of culture, and especially in attempts to train them to perform processes of which they do not understand the theory, the only chance of success lies in making them repeat, incessantly, certain acts in an invariable order.

By this incessant repetition you will create a habit, and by the invariableness of the order you educate, that feebleness of the memory for unfamiliar facts, which almost always accompanies deficiency of mental training.

Therefore if anybody desires to train an ignorant girl to wait at table, she must be made to do the same thing every day in the same sequence, and with no omission or departure from the programme. This is, however, rarely put into practice—but the common way is to exact from the girl the least possible service when the family are by themselves, but when guests are present a number of new duties are put upon her, for which she sees no reason, and cannot possibly keep them in mind.

The result is that the attention of the lady of the house is entirely absorbed in the servant, to the neglect of her friends, and she is obliged to give orders continually, while the well-meaning girl becomes so confused, that she cannot even change a plate properly, and the dinner is not a success; and the mistress learns that constant drilling is needful to make a raw girl a good waitress.

A girl cannot be expected to become an accomplished cook, waitress, or chamber-maid, until she has passed several years in the various occupations, each position requires. And when she first sees the dinner table of a family, who live in moderate style, it must seem to her somewhat like the preparation of a mysterious heathen rite.

The rules and regulations which control the laying of the table, the course of the dishes, the changing of the plates, etc., are provisions for the gratification of tastes, for which only years of training will fit her. She cannot understand why the eating of a meal should be surrounded by so much elaboration and ceremony; and any explanation of the theory would not be satisfactory, because it is chiefly founded upon ideas which need a high system of cultivation.

To endeavor to make a waitress feel about the service at table as her mistress does, that is, to give her the mistress' sense of propriety, decency and fitness would be an utter impossibility.—*The Nation.*

The Best Way to Labor Easily.

A scholar may be able to write in a dogged manner, with a determined resolution to grind out a given task at all hazards. So a person may put whip and spur to his overworked and dragged out energies, and engage in manual employment as the sullen culprit goes scourged to his irksome labor.

If one must sit with pen already dipped, and woo his ideas and tumble his dictionary for suggestive words, he will be very apt to write and erase, to change and alter repeatedly, before the sluggish thoughts can be satisfactorily expressed.

Thus it is also with manual labor; if one cannot engage in it as a buoyant urchin bounds away to the play-ground, everything will drag heavily. If the thoughts do not come rushing across the orbit of the mind in rapid succession, as the fleet shadows of Summer clouds chase each other over the landscape, throw aside the pen, touch not the newspaper or book, but take a brisk walk into town or country. Throw aside all care and thoughtfulness, let down the tension which has held the entire system at concert pitch for so many days, and try to feel that you have nothing to do for at least three weeks.

Then, after an invigorative pause, dip the pen again, and the well-arranged thoughts will flow as smoothly as the ink.

After writing an hour, drop the pen, no matter if in the midst of a sentence, and recreate for ten or fifteen minutes by your watch; after which resume it. Always exercising rigid attention over self, to stop entirely before the monitor within says that every faculty has been overworked.

A manual laborer who will apply himself faithfully for eight or ten successive hours, with an hour's intermission, will accomplish more and feel better than if he worked along for ten hours without any rest.

The housekeeper who would perform a great day's work, without overdoing, must stop and rest a little every hour or two. A person can accomplish but little, who is ever hurrying and always behindhand; but if he will sit down or lie idle for an hour, labor would not seem so irksome, and when the clock indicated that the hour of rest was passed, she would be surprised to see what a pleasure there is in virtuous industry, and how much she can accomplish when she is not so tired. The great difficulty with most housekeepers is over doing, and she who goads her already overtaxed energies, hour after hour, in all the endless round of house-work, will often find, too late, perhaps, that she has been burning the candle at both ends.

It is not the great amount of work in the aggregate which prostrates the physical and mental powers, but it is the habit of tiring one's self in the performance of every task, and never feeling wholly rested, when one rises in the morning.

False Motions.

It is not always those who seem the most occupied, who can accomplish the most work; and this fact is forcibly illustrated by the following incident:

The foreman of one of our large newspaper establishments was showing a stranger over the office. In the composing-room he saw with wonder and admiration the thousands of little bits of metal passing with a steady click, click, into the sticks which the workmen held. As he watched them the foreman asked him which of the compositors he thought could do the most work.

He replied, "Why, that tall fellow in the corner sets twice as many types as the others. His hands fly with great rapidity."

"No," answered the foreman, "our fastest type-setter is that quiet-looking man opposite."

"He seems very slow and moderate in his movements," said the stranger. "His motions are not nearly so quick as the one I pointed out."

"It is true," said the foreman, "but the secret is that he never fails to pick the right letter, while the other makes what we call 'false motions.' His hand goes twice to the case for a type, and his stick fills slowly compared with that of the deliberate workman, who does not hurry, and uses only just enough action to accomplish his purpose."

"*False motions*" are the cause of a great amount of wasted energy; and there are many housewives who suffer greatly from that fault. They dash about the house and seem to be working at a great rate, but they rarely accomplish much, while the women who do their work deliberately and slowly, taking time to consider what should be done next, to the best advantage, will accomplish more in half a day than they can do in a day, and not become so much exhausted.

Think more about your work, and take it easy. It's always best to take things in a quiet sort of way.

Keep cool; don't fume and fret, but consider how a thing should be done, and do it, thus avoiding "false motions," and letting every step tell, and every move an advance towards the completion of the work.

Teach your children to do work in this manner, and it will often prove the best legacy you can give them.

How to Enjoy Life.

It is lamentable to what a degree many persons believe that enjoyment and contentment depend upon not being obliged to engage in constant occupations.

Nowadays, girls are considered well settled in life, if their husbands possess sufficient means to provide them with plenty of servants, and place them in the enviable position of nothing to do.

While young men are thought to be well provided for if their parents possess large fortunes, and can furnish them with sufficient capital to either play at business, by sitting in the counting-room or office, and letting others do the work, or to give them funds to make the grand tour, and go up to the head-waters of the Nile.

Now this is all nonsense, for honest, hearty labor is the only true source of happiness, as well as the only guarantee of health and life.

"By the sweat of thy brow thou shalt eat thy bread," was the divine command to Adam. And whoever is so unfortunate as to have nothing to do in the grand arena of life, is sure to suffer from disobedience to it.

Work is essential for every one, and without its incentives, without we pay heed to its claims upon us, we are miserable misanthropes, and the gloom of misanthropy is not only an hindrance to all enjoyment, but it tends to destroy life itself.

For luxury and idleness lead to premature decay much more surely than many occupations that are considered fatal to longevity.

As a general thing, instead of labor shortening our lives, it actually increases them, and it is for the want of occupation that so many of our rich men's sons become dissipated and insane, and their daughters querulous invalids.

The drones of life are subject to all sorts of diseases, which prove utter kill-joys, and it is only the busy bees who enjoy the sunshine and the flowers of life.

INDEX TO PART I.

	PAGE.
Alabaster, restore ornaments in,	12
A good plan for a kitchen,	105
Ammonia, its uses,	78
Antidote to poison,	56
Ants, the plague of,	26
Apartments, arrangement of,	61
A revolving fire grate,	92
Ashes, a plea for,	61
Aquariums, water-proof cement,	39
A use for old corks,	48
A wash to fix pencil drawings,	47
Blacking, sponge boot,	49
Blankets, how to wash,	34
Brass andirons and fenders, how to clean,	10
Beds, to clean bedding and,	20
Beds, how to air,	24
Bedsteads, to re-paint iron,	125
Bread, how to prepare stale,	42
Borax, the use of,	29
Books, how to lend and borrow,	53
Borrowing,	81
Bottles, remove stopper from smelling,	10
Bottles, remove stopper from glass,	10
Burns and scalds,	55
Bluing, recipe for,	30
Brushes to cleanse hair and clothes,	51
Calcimine,	88
Candlesticks, to clean snuffers and,	12
Carpets, how to lay,	113
Carpets, how to make rag,	124
Care of family stores,	121
Care of woolen curtains,	50
Care of pictures,	50
Carpet, to make a cheap,	23
Chamber, how to ventilate,	44
Crape, to restore,	45
Cellar, how to clean,	19
Cellar, to ventilate,	47
Cement, water-proof,	39
Cement, lime and egg,	40
Cement, rice-flour,	41
Cement, fire and water-proof,	41
Cement for the mouth of bottles,	75
Cisterns, how to build,	55
China, how to mend,	39
Coat, to renovate a black,	60
Coral, to make black, white, or red frames,	47
Corks, a use for old,	48
Clothing to disinfect,	49
Clock, how to fix the,	141
Clothes, how to brush,	123
Crockery, white lead for mending,	40
Curtains, to do up lace,	36
Curtains, care of woolen,	50
Dampness, how to prevent,	122
Drawings, a wash to fix,	47
Dress making, hints on,	27
Doors, to prevent creaking,	67
Don't shut out the sunshine,	97
Dusters, home made feather,	90
Earthen ware, management of,	52
Engravings to transfer on wood,	71
Expenses, how to manage household,	14
Economy, home,	14
Facts for housekeepers,	141
False motions,	150
Flannels, how to wash,	35

INDEX.

	PAGE.
Flannels,	28
Fermentation, facts about,	89
Freckles, to remove,	42
Filtered water,	56
Finger nails, to cure children from biting their,	145
Fire-guard made of wire,	46
Fire, to extinguish fires in chimneys,	59
Fire, how to extinguish clothes on fire,	79
Flies, to destroy,	42
Friendship,	140
Floors, to wash,	21
Furniture, polish for,	49
Furs, how to take care of,	25
Glasses, how to clean,	86
Grease, to remove spots from books,	44
Grease, to extract from silk,	45
Gold, how to restore French gold ornaments,	54
Gloves, how to buy,	44
Gloves, to clean Doeskin,	51
Gloves, to clean white kid,	51
Gloves, to restore black kid,	52
Glue, Burgardien's,	40
Glue for constant use,	41
Hair, how to crimp,	67
Hair wash,	43
Harness, to restore faded,	13
Harness, Castor oil for,	86
Hearth to black a brick,	43
Hints for the Laundry,	29
Hints on varnishing,	127
Hints upon moving,	112
Home interests,	92
Honor your occupation,	144
House, how to purify,	42
Houses, best time for painting,	141
House cleaning, how to arrange the spring,	15
Housekeeping,	110
House linen, hints upon,	106
How much to eat,	68
How to build a cistern,	55
How to crimp the hair,	67

	PAGE.
How to clean knives,	69
How to clean wall paper and walls,	17
How to clean a room thoroughly,	16
How to clean carpets,	16
How to cultivate the habit of reading,	116
How to destroy flies,	42
How to drive,	82
How to dry herbs,	69
How to hang pictures,	70
How to enjoy life,	151
How to iron,	34
How to iron skirts, vests and shirts,	31
How to mend old boots and shoes,	58
How to mend old pails,	69
How to make a comfortable home,	96
How to make new rope pliable,	68
How to make home happy,	65
How to make a storm glass,	59
How to make a model village,	148
How to make a wire fire-guard,	46
How to mend sheets and shirts,	45
How to pack household articles,	76
How to prevent cold feet,	71
How to prepare tracing paper,	48
How to pour out tea,	138
How to restore faded alpaca,	55
How to remove mildew,	50
How to sleep,	53
How to store fruit for winter use,	57
How to teach little children,	118
How to utilize old cans,	131
How to use French polish,	129
How to use kerosene lamps,	62
How to use old carpets,	23
How to ventilate rooms and large halls,	72
How to ventilate cellar,	47
How to wash fine under clothing,	136
How to wash old flannels,	39
Ice house, an extemporaneous,	132
Inks, sympathetic,	48
Ink for marking linen,	49
Ink stains, to remove,	45
Ironing,	34
Iron rust, to extract from linen,	61

INDEX.

	PAGE.
Ivy poison, remedy for,	57
Javelle water for stains,	79
Knives, to clean,	69
Knives, to take care of handles of,	11
Lace, to bleach embroidery and,	33
Lace, to wash thread,	44
Laces and muslins, to wash,	30
Linen, ink for marking,	49
Linen, care of house linen,	126
Linen, to remove fruit stains from,	36
Linen, to renew scorched,	76
Linen, to restore mildewed,	36
Linen, to stiffen,	33
Linen, to take out iron rust,	61
Lamps, to use kerosene,	62
Mahogany, to extracts ink spots,	45
Management of earthen ware,	52
Mats made of sheepskin,	69
Matting, how to put down,	223
Matting, how to wash straw,	139
Mildew, how to remove,	150
Mosquito and fly nets,	24
Muslin dresses, how to wash,	32
Moths, how to repel,	24
Needlework, plain,	28
Open windows at night,	133
Overcoats, hints on repairing,	134
Oil cloths, to clean,	21
Oil cloth, to protect edges of,	22
Oil cloth, to make a kitchen,	22
Our boys,	93
Our children,	92
Our homes,	95
Paint impervious to weather,	13
Paint, to remove from cloth,	43
Paint, to make economical white,	13
Patching and darning,	73
Plate, to clean tarnished,	12
Plate, to clean,	66
Plated goods, to restore,	44
Plaster figures, to clean,	60
Plaster, to give the appearance of marble to figures in,	12
Pictures, appropriateness of,	103
Pictures, care of,	50
Pictures and chromos, how to clean,	21
Pimples, remove from the face,	43
Prints, to wash black and white,	34
Poison, antidotes for,	56
Poison by ivy, remedy for,	53
Polish, French,	128
Polish, to apply French,	66
Polish for furniture	49
Polishing paste for tins, etc.,	46
Pomade, how to make,	79
Pot Pourri No. 1,	9
Pot Pourri No. 2,	10
Refrigerator, a home made,	26
Roses, how to make the otto of,	81
Rug, to make a rag,	62
Rugs out of old carpets,	89
Rust, to preserve iron and steel,	11
Sachet powders,	45
Scalp, to cleanse,	43
Scrap book, the value of,	132
Stains from silver,	42
Starch made from coffee,	33
Stains, to remove fruit,	60
Stains, how to remove stains from clothing,	90
Servants, how to train,	148
Sleeping rooms, comfort in,	98
Sheets and shirts, how to mend,	45
Silk, to clean,	67
Silk, to extract grease from,	45
Silver, East Indian method of cleaning,	87
Silver, to remove egg stains,	42
Silver, to prepare cloths for polishing,	12
Simplicity in living,	94
Shirt making, directions for,	109
Shirts, vests and skirts to iron,	31
Skin, how to whiten,	121
Soap for scrubbing,	38
Soap, to make pure white,	38
Soap, to make hard,	37
Soap without ashes,	37
Soap dish, a convenient,	32
Soap making, hints upon,	36
Shopping, hints on,	115

INDEX.

	PAGE.
Stockings, to wash silk,	43
Stockings, to wash black woolen,	33
Storm glass, how to make,	59
Sympathetic inks for writing,	48
The art of color,	105
The charm of reserve,	146
The fine art of patching,	73
The rag bag,	137
The use of paper in the house,	134
Time, how to economize,	120
Tins, to clean common,	11
Tins, Britannia ware, polish for,	46
To black-lead and polish grates,	18
To clean colored fabrics,	31
To clean colored and varnished paints,	19
To clean Doeskin gloves,	51
To clean door knobs, bell pulls,	21
To clean glasses, bottles, decanters,	67
To clean marble,	74
To clean wash leather gloves,	52
To clean white kid gloves,	51
To clean wainscots and painted wood,	19
To clean white paint,	18
To clean waiters,	77
To close cracks in stoves,	85
To cut pencils for drawing,	64
To disinfect clothing by sulphur,	49
To keep leather harness pliable,	75
To make black, red, or white coral frames,	47
To make a rag rug,	62
To prevent hair falling off,	67
To perfume linen,	74
To preserve steel ornaments,	64
To remove freckles,	42
To remove grease from carpets, table-cloths, dresses,	46
To remove ink stains,	45
To remove iron rust,	137
To remove stains from the fingers,	74
To restore black kid gloves,	52
To restore crape,	45
To restore woolen furniture,	60
To stain woods,	50
To wash cretonne and chintz,	126
To wash laces and muslins,	30
To wash muslin dresses,	32
To wash ribbons, silk handkerchiefs,	75
To wash vials,	76
Towels, to repair,	44
To ventilate closets,	129
Varnish, old straw hats and baskets,	13
Velvet, to iron,	76
Venetian blinds, to clean,	22
Vials, how to wash,	76
Washing fluid,	29
Wash, black and blue linens,	35
Water-proof boots and shoes,	57
Water-proof boots,	86
Windows, to clean mirrors and,	21
Window draperies,	82
Wines, how to know if colored,	122
Whitewash, a recipe for,	80
Whitewashing, directions for,	87
White lead for mending crockery,	40
Woods, to stain,	50
Woolen, Scotch method of washing shawls,	136
Why girls should be taught to keep house,	114

Ladies' Fancy Work,
OR
HOME RECREATIONS
IN
Art & Household Taste.

Just published, a Charming New Book with above title. A Companion Volume to

Household Elegancies and Window Gardening,

Issued in same size and style, profusely illustrated with engravings of superior execution, and devoted to many topics of Household taste, Fancy Work for the ladies, and containing hundreds of suggestions of Home decorations.

VOLUME THREE

OF

Williams' Household Series.

CONTENTS.

Among the topics which "Ladies' Fancy Work" treats of, are—
Feather Work, Paper Flowers, Fire Screens, Shrines, Rustic Pictures, a charming series of designs for Easter Crosses, Straw Ornaments, Shell Flowers and Shell Work, Bead Mosaic, and Fish Scale Embroidery, Hair Work, Card-board Ornaments, Fancy Rubber Work, Cottage Foot Rests, Window Garden Decorations, Crochet Work, designs in Embroidery, and an immense number of designs of other Fancy Work to delight all lovers of Household Art and recreation.
Price sent post-paid by mail, $1.50.

Address, HENRY T. WILLIAMS, Publisher,

P. O. Box 6,205.   46 Beekman Street, New York.

HOUSEHOLD ELEGANCIES.

The most beautiful Ladies' Book ever published. Get it for your Work Basket or Parlor. A Beautiful Gift to Friends.

BY HENRY T. WILLIAMS AND MRS. C. S. JONES.

VOL. 2—WILLIAMS' HOUSEHOLD SERIES.

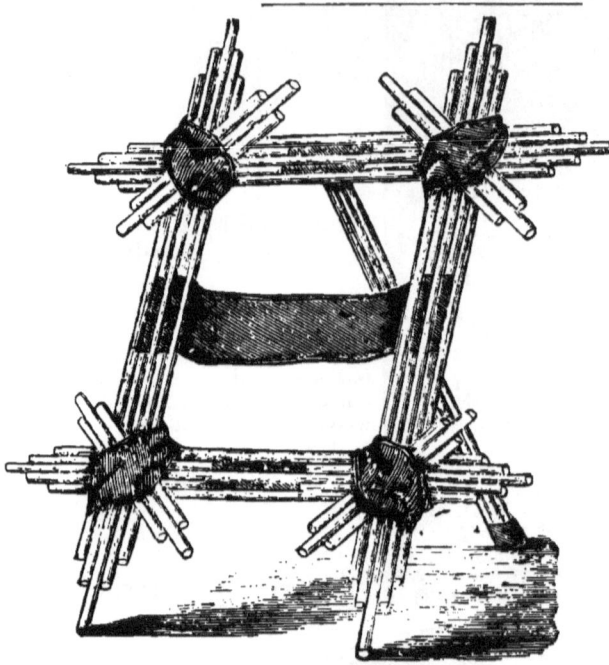

A splendid new book on Household Art, devoted to a multitude of topics, interesting to ladies everywhere.

CONTENTS.

Chap. 1—Transparencies on Glass for Windows, Lamps, Halls, etc.—Diaphanie, Vitremanie. 18 Engravings.
Chap. 2—Fancy Work with Leaves, Flowers and Grasses —Phantom Leaves, Autumn Leaves and Mosses. 23 Engravings.
Chap. 3—Spray Work or Spatter Work. 23 Engravings.
Chap. 4—Brackets, Shelves, Mantels, etc. 27 Engravings.
Chap. 5—Picture Frames — 17 Engravings.
Chap. 6—Fancy Leather Work. 29 Engravings.
Chap. 7—Wall Pockets. 18 Engravings.
Chap. 8—Work Boxes and Baskets. 17 Engravings.
Chap. 9—Wax Flowers, Fruit, etc. 21 Engravings.
Chap. 10—Indian Painting in imitation of Ebony and Ivory. 14 Engravings.
Chap. 11—Cone, Spruce and Seed Work. 35 Engravings.
Chap. 12—Miscellaneous Fancy Work. 46 Engravings.

Hundreds of exquisite illustrations decorate the pages, which are full to overflowing with hints and devices to every lady, how to ornament her home cheaply, tastefully and delightfully, with fancy articles of her own construction. By far the most popular and elegant gift book of the year—300 pages. Price $1.50. Sent post-paid by mail.

P. O. Box 6205.   ADDRESS HENRY T. WILLIAMS, PUBLISHER,
46 BEEKMAN STREET, NEW YORK.

Window Gardening.

By HENRY T. WILLIAMS,

Editor Ladies' Floral Cabinet N. Y.

RICHLY ILLUSTRATED WITH EXQUISITE ENGRAVINGS.

An Elegant Book, with 250 Fine Engravings and 300 Pages,

Containing a Descriptive List of all Plants Suitable for Window Culture.

A ready and invaluable aid to all who wish to adorn their houses in the easiest and most successful manner with plants or vines, or flowers. Instructions are given as to the best selection of plants for Baskets or Ferneries and Wardian Cases. Several chapters are devoted to Hanging Baskets, Climbing Vines, Smilax, and the Ivy, for decorative purposes. Bulbs for House Culture are fully described; also ornamental Plants for Dinner Table Decoration. Other topics are well considered, such as Balcony Gardens, House Top Gardening, Watering Plants, Home Conservatories, Fountains, Vases, Flower Stands, Soil, Air, Temperature, Propagation, Floral Boxes, the Aquarium, Rustic Conveniences for Household Ornament, and directions in detail for the general management of in-door plants for the entire year throughout the Winter, Spring, Summer and Fall. The volume is profusely illustrated with choice engravings, and pains have been taken to make it one of the most attractive books ever issued, from the American Press. For sale or supplied by Bookstores everywhere, or sent post-paid by mail on receipt of price.

Price, $1.50.

Every Woman Her Own Flower Gardener.

By Daisy Eyebright, (Mrs. S. O. Johnson,)

A delightful little volume, written by a lady fond of flowers, as a special help and assistance to others interested in out door flower gardening. Simple directions are given, how to lay out and plant Flower Borders, Ribbon Beds, and arrange ornamental plants. Among the topics treated are Geraniums, Fuchsias, Bulbs Ornamental Flowering Shrubs, Everlasting Flowers, Ornamental Grasses, Coleus, Paeonies, Shade Trees, Garden Vegetables, Old Fashioned Flowers, Annual Flowers, Perennials, Ornamental Vines, Lawns, Insects, Manures, Watering Soils, When and How to Plant, Dahlias, Lilies, Gladiolus, Verbenas, Cannas, Balsams, Portulaccas, and nearly all the popular varieties of flowers and shrubs. The book contains 148 pages, is charmingly written by one deeply in love with the subject, who appreciates the tastes of ladies and aims to do good with agreeable, kindly advice on home gardening. For sale or supplied by Bookstores everywhere.

Price, in handsome Pamphlet Covers, 50 cents; bound in Cloth, $1; postpaid by mail.

Address **HENRY T. WILLIAMS,** *Publisher,*

46 Beekman Street, N. Y.

Ornamental Designs
—FOR—
Fret-Work, Scroll Sawing, Fancy Carving,
—AND—
HOME DECORATIONS.

Fret-Sawing has become an art of such wonderful popularity that the interest in it has been shared by both amateurs and professionals to an astonishing extent. Hundreds are earning large sums of pocket-money by cutting these beautiful household ornaments, and selling among friends or acquaintances, or at the art stores.

Ladies and the Young Folks find in it a fascinating recreation, and are making dozens of fancy articles at small cost, to decorate their homes in a charming manner, or to give as Holiday Presents to friends. The following books contain mechanical designs of full size for immediate use, and are invaluable alike to the amateurs, ladies, young folks, mechanics, architects, and all of professional skill.

PART 1 contains full size designs for Picture Frames, Small Brackets, Book Racks, Fancy Letters and Figures, Ornaments, Wall Pockets, etc. (Has patterns worth at usual prices over $8.) Price, 75 cts., post-paid by mail.

PART 2 is devoted exclusively to designs of Brackets of medium to large size, all entirely new, and of the most tasteful detail and execution. (Contains over 50 plans, worth at least $15.) Price $1.00, by mail, post-paid.

PART 3 is devoted to Fancy Work, Ladies' Work Baskets, Easels, Crosses, Match Boxes, Pen Racks, Paper Cutters, Calendar Frames, Thermometer Stands, Watch Pockets, Fruit Baskets, Table Platters, etc. Nearly 100 designs, many of them really exquisite. Price, $1.

The above books contain over 300 patterns, all beautifully printed in blue color. These books are the only ones yet issued in the U. S. The patterns are mostly original, designed expressly for these books, and in execution, choice selection, taste, cheapness, they may be safely esteemed the best collection yet produced! The whole series of three costing but $2.75, contains upwards of 300 patterns, worth at usual values over $30. All sent post-paid by mail, on receipt of price.

Bracket and Fret Saw.

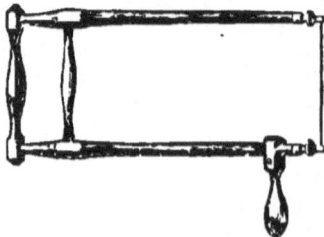

With this Bracket Saw, the designs and directions, very desirable articles can be made for Fairs, etc., which will sell quickly and at a good profit. With it you can *make beautiful articles for presentation gifts.* With it you can *help beautify your homes.* With it you can *make money.* To parents desiring a USEFUL GIFT for their children, we would call attention to this Bracket and Fret Saw, for it not only affords *great pleasure, but it helps to cultivate a mechanical taste.*

Price with 25 bracket and ornamental designs, 6 bracket saw blades, also full directions for use. Sent by mail for $1.25.

Address HENRY T. WILLIAMS, Publisher,
46 Beekman Street, New York.

Part 4, Price 50 Cents.—A new book of Fret Saw designs, containing many tasteful patterns, entirely new and of special elegance, is now in press, and will be issued early in October.

www.ingramcontent.com/pod-product-compliance
Lightning Source LLC
Chambersburg PA
CBHW030302170426
43202CB00009B/847